101
WAYS TO MARKET
YOUR BUSINESS

ALSO BY ANDREW GRIFFITHS

101 Ways to Really Satisfy Your Customers
101 Ways to Boost Your Business
101 Ways to Advertise Your Business
Secrets to Building a Winning Business

COMING SOON

101 Ways to Balance Your Business and Your Life
101 Ways to Network Marketing

101 WAYS TO ADVERTISE YOUR BUSINESS

Read this before you spend another cent on advertising

Here are 101 proven tips to increase the effectiveness of your advertising. Use these tips to understand what makes one ad work while another fails and you will save a small fortune in wasted advertising.

With tips designed to take just a few moments to read, *101 Ways to Advertise Your Business* offers step-by-step advice on how to make an advertisement, how to buy advertising space and how to make sure that your advertisement is working to its full potential. Follow the tips and your business will soon be reaping the benefits.

INCLUDES A SPECIAL BONUS SECTION CONTAINING HUNDREDS OF THE BEST ADVERTISING WORDS AND PHRASES

101
WAYS TO MARKET YOUR BUSINESS

ANDREW GRIFFITHS

ALLEN&UNWIN

First published in 2000
This edition published in 2006

Allen & Unwin
83 Alexander Street
Crows Nest NSW 2065
Australia
Phone: (61 2) 8425 0100
Fax: (61 2) 9906 2218
Email: info@allenandunwin.com
Web: www.allenandunwin.com

National Library of Australia
Cataloguing-in-Publication entry:

Griffiths, Andrew, 1966– .
   101 ways to market your business.
   ISBN 978 1 74175 005 8.

   ISBN 1 74175 005 9.

   1. Marketing – Australia – Handbooks, manuals, etc. 2.
   Small business – Australia – Marketing. I. Title.

658.8020994

Set in 12/14 pt Adobe Garamond by Midland Typesetters, Australia
Printed in Australia by McPherson's Printing Group

10 9 8 7 6 5 4 3 2 1

Contents

Acknowledgments

I would like to thank the people who have encouraged and assisted me with this book. I have always been an optimist; I believe it to be my greatest asset. However, without the support and enthusiasm of friends and family a dream such as writing a book can easily go unrealised.

First, my sister, Wendy Bateson. Success is measured in many ways but I have no doubt that Wendy was the most successful person I have ever known. Most of my drive and all of my ambition are thanks to her.

Also, my business friends and colleagues of the past 20 years. I feel somewhat guilty that you have all given me so much for so little in return. For that I thank you from the bottom of my heart. I hope that the information and experiences relayed in this book will go on to help many others. By the way, I'm sorry for not ringing for the past few years – I've been busy.

1 | **Getting started**

People generally start a small business or buy a small business for different reasons. Sometimes it is because they are good at their chosen profession and feel that they can make a better living working for themselves, sometimes it is a lifestyle change and sometimes it is simply a lifelong dream.

With the advent of retrenchment and redundancy packages or early retirement payouts there are many more people facing retirement long before they are actually ready. They have cash and they have the energy and enthusiasm to start their own business. The problem is that they rarely have the experience required to run their new venture and to make money.

Running a business requires many skills that take time to develop. The question is how much time do you have to develop them?

We are often reminded that many small businesses fail within the first few years. From my experience the two main reasons are a lack of initial capital (not enough money) and a lack of marketing ability. The people running these businesses work very hard, generally have excellent products and often are completely dedicated to making their business a success, but they just don't know how to find new customers or keep existing ones.

So where do you turn for marketing advice? You can engage the services of a marketing consultant to help develop specialist marketing plans and to give you plenty of ideas and suggestions on ways to attract more business. This is what thousands of marketing consultants, including myself, do around the world every day. Generally our clients are larger firms that have the budget to call in specialist advice.

However, the vast majority of businesses are small one- or two-person operations that have very limited funds. They can't afford to have their own marketing consultant on call. Their needs are more immediate and their resources, including time and money, are generally limited.

The upside to this is that most of these small businesses normally only need a gentle nudge in the right direction to produce dramatic improvements in their business. Based on this need I decided to write this book. My dream was to create a clear, easy-to-read manual that any business operator could pick up and start using immediately. I wanted to offer a lot of simple marketing ideas that were tried and tested. They had to be logical, easy to implement and affordable.

The ideas and strategies suggested do not require any special skills and they will not take up a lot of your time. Business operators want to be able to do things straight away, not plan for ten years' time. If business is quiet they want to be able to do something about it immediately. This book will provide the opportunity to be proactive about marketing today.

Marketing ideas are important for success; however, I also believe that having the right attitude is essential. I have been fortunate enough to work with a lot of very successful business operators. They all have similar attitudes and thoughts on doing business and I believe that is what sets them apart from those businesses that always seem to struggle. I have included many suggestions that are based on my observations of these very successful business operators.

If the ideas and suggestions detailed in this book help just one business to stop struggling and to become successful, I will be a very happy man.

How to get results fast using this book

Most business books offer chapter after chapter of complex information, graphs and catchy buzz words that you need to work your way through before you can get started. Not this one. If you are getting edgy and you want to get started turn to the 101 Marketing Ideas section (page 27) and go for it. Choose an idea that you like the look of and get started today.

The best way to get results fast is to implement a new idea each week, depending on your budget and the time that you allocate to marketing your business. If you can implement one idea per week, you will have initiated fifty new marketing ideas within a year, each one generating more income for your business.

If you want more information about the ideas and the philosophy behind the simple marketing ideas discussed in this book, go to the introductory section 'What do you need to know to get started?' (page 4). This section outlines some of the ideas and philosophies behind marketing any business.

Some ideas and themes are repeated throughout the book. The reason for this is that they are very important issues that really need to be emphasised to improve your chances of success. The other reason is that this book has been designed to offer practical marketing ideas on virtually every page. Some ideas need a little background to illustrate the point that I am trying to make, so don't look at it as a repeat, look at it as me nagging.

There are also a number of sample forms that illustrate the ideas suggested. These can be found at the back of the book. One of the most important forms is the 'Marketing activity report'. Basically all you need to do is fill in the blanks as you start on a new idea and then update it as results start coming in. Put them in a file and you will have an accurate and detailed account of your company's marketing activities. This will prove to be an asset the day that you decide to sell your business as you can show prospective buyers exactly what you have done to promote the business.

What do you need to know to get started?

This part of the book is designed to give you a broad overview of marketing any business. It will provide the answers to many of the commonly asked questions and it will provide these answers in a simple, easy to understand format.

The questions that will be answered and the topics covered include:

- how much time you should spend marketing your business;
- how much money you should spend on marketing;
- why it is important to understand your customers;
- what type of promotional material you should be using;
- ways to stay motivated; and
- tips for running a successful business.

I recommend that you read this part at some stage, whether before or after you have read the 101 Marketing Ideas. The information contained in the next few pages forms the basis of the marketing advice I give to all of my clients. Without a doubt it helps to build successful businesses.

How much time do you need to devote to marketing?

Most of the marketing ideas recommended in this book will take less than 30 minutes to implement. The big question that you need to ask yourself is how much time can you devote to marketing and promoting your business? You may be able to spend 30 minutes per month or you may be fired up and ready to commit to 30 minutes per day. It doesn't matter how much time you allocate as long as you make the effort to implement new ideas on a regular basis. You be the judge on how regular the basis needs to be.

The time that you devote to marketing your business needs to be quality time. It is no good trying to squeeze it in among the thousand and one other responsibilities that you have to deal with on a daily basis. I am a firm believer in doing your marketing away from your business, in an environment where you won't be disturbed or distracted. At least use this time to plan your strategy and then do the actual implementing of ideas at the office.

Many business operators feel that marketing is like doing book work—it is something that you have to do rather than something that you want to do. We all know what happens if you don't do your book work. At the end of the financial year you sheepishly take the shoe box full of receipts to the accountant who gives you 'the look'. You throw the box on the accountant's desk and run out the door. A few months later the tax man rings asking a few 'please explain' type questions and eventually you will have to pay someone a lot of money.

Not doing your marketing on a regular basis can have a more dramatic end result—your business goes broke. The moral is simple—you need to be disciplined and you need to set aside a realistic amount of time to market your business on a regular basis.

How much business do you need to survive?

This is the start to any marketing campaign or plan and unfortunately it is seldom considered in small businesses. You need to ask yourself the question: how much business do I really need?

There are two reasons to ask this question. The first is to give you a daily target to aim for. If you don't know how much business you want you will never be satisfied. The other reason is to try to eliminate the risk of getting too much business—yes, that's right, too much business.

The important thing to do now is to take a few minutes and work out exactly how much business you need to cover all of your costs. Be honest and realistic and overestimate rather than underestimate. You can work out this figure for a year, a month, a week or a day. I like to work it out on a monthly basis, as most of our customers pay once per month.

Once you know exactly how much business you need to cover all costs you know exactly how much business you need to survive. This is what it will cost you to open the doors every day.

The next step is to decide how much profit you want to make from your business. Add this to your survival figure and, presto, you now have a figure to aim for. This tells you exactly how much business you want.

It is amazing how clear everything becomes when all of

a sudden you know how much business you need to survive and how much business you want to make a profit. Very few businesses take the time to figure these targets out, but successful ones always do.

The second point, generating too much business, brings to mind the following stories. A friend of mine was involved in building a large oceanarium. The launch of the attraction was very big with hundreds of thousands of dollars spent on enticing crowds for the opening day. Well the crowds came—far more than the oceanarium had allowed for—and the result was that the day was a disaster. People were stuck in queues for hours, the crush of the crowds was crazy, the restaurants ran out of food, children were lost, people fainted and so on.

It took a long time for this attraction to rebuild its reputation. The grand opening was a financial success but a complete failure in terms of long-term marketing. The crowds left after a disappointing experience and consequently they told their family and friends not to bother visiting the attraction because it was a shambles.

Another short story that I have found fascinating has to do with smoking. A friend recently tried to stop smoking following an intensive advertising campaign from the QUIT line (a number people could call for advice and support to quit smoking) on television. The graphic blood and gore advertisements were too much and the QUIT line seemed to be a fabulous support for anyone trying to give up the dreaded nicotine. The advertisement worked and my friend made the decision to quit on the spot.

After a week without cigarettes she had a moment of weakness and decided that she needed help quickly—no problems. A quick call to the QUIT line and everything will be OK. She called the line, was put on hold for ten minutes and then a rather rude lady said that she couldn't help now but someone would call back soon.

Seven days later someone called, apologising about the delay and protesting that the extra advertising had made them so busy that they could not cope with the thousands of calls they were getting every day. By this stage my friend had given up trying to quit and she still smokes.

There is a valuable lesson to be learned. If you start to do a lot of marketing make certain that your business can cope with the increase. All businesses want the phone to be running hot but few can cope with a sudden increase in business without making at least a few operational changes. New customers that come to your business as a result of your marketing activity will be testing you to see if you can deliver what you promise. If you don't impress them the first time around you may never get the opportunity to try again.

Why is it important to be different?

Imagine if you had a dose of the flu and you decided that you needed to buy some medicine. Imagine you go to the shops and find ten individual pharmacies next door to each other, all in a nice neat row and basically all the same. How do you decide which pharmacy to purchase your flu medication from? Do you look for the cheapest, the one with the most helpful staff, the biggest, the smallest, the longest established, the one that you have visited before or simply the one closest? These are the kinds of questions that we subconsciously ask every time we go to purchase an item.

The big question is: what makes your business different from your competitors? If your customers are trying to choose between your business and your competitors' businesses, why should they use yours? You need to come up with the answer to this question and it needs to be convincing.

Several years ago the very famous company Federal Express found themselves struggling in the highly competitive world of freight. They decided that they needed a policy or a statement to explain why people should use their impressive range of freight services, which were basically the same as every other freight courier in the USA.

The advertising agency came up with the slogan, 'If it absolutely, positively has to be there overnight use Federal Express'. A large campaign was launched to promote this new company slogan and the rest is history. Federal Express has grown to become one of the largest freight companies in the world. The main reason attributed to the success of this slogan is the fact that it identified what makes Federal Express different from their numerous competitors by stating that if it really needs to get there you had better use Federal Express. It implies that if your package really has to get where it is going by tomorrow, Federal Express are the only ones that can get it there.

Some of the most effective words to use when trying to come up with one simple slogan that will differentiate your business from your competitors are the biggest, the largest, the longest established, the freshest, the best, the most, guaranteed, the perfect, the finest, the leading, the right, the highest and the foremost.

The one thing that is certain in business is that competition will continue to increase. There will be more people trying to sell similar items to the same number of people. For this reason it is important to identify what makes your business different to and, ultimately, better than your competitors.

How much money do you need to spend on marketing?

Finding the money to market and advertise a business is often not easy. When times are tough people tend to cut back in the area of advertising—this is the time that advertising and marketing should be increased but it rarely happens that way.

Most businesses that come to me for advice have very limited budgets—sometimes as little as $20 per week. My advice is always the same. The size of the budget doesn't matter but how you use it does. It is all relative. A company with a $20 per week marketing budget probably needs to generate a few thousand dollars per year. A company with a million dollar marketing budget needs to turn over tens of millions per year.

Determining how much money you should spend promoting your business is a difficult decision. The accepted way to arrive at a marketing budget is a percentage of your total turnover, anywhere from 5 per cent to 20 per cent. If the figure you picked was 10 per cent and you turn over a million dollars a year, you are planning on spending $100 000 per year in advertising and marketing.

It is always wise to talk to your accountant or financial advisor when it comes to setting a budget, but remember, marketing should be a fixed cost like rent or electricity. If you don't actively promote your business it will soon disappear. If you wait until you are desperate you are under a lot more pressure to get the results.

I recently had a jeweller approach me to do some marketing for his company. He had been operating for over fifteen years and he had never spent a cent on marketing. This man was very successful but in the last five years competition had increased, tourist numbers had dropped and business had suddenly got tough. He was very humble and it was obvious that he had done a lot of soul searching to understand why his business was failing. His greatest realisation was that he didn't take an active stance in marketing his business because he thought that the customers would always be there.

Having said that, don't feel that you need to have a

marketing budget of hundreds of thousands of dollars to produce results. There are thousands of small businesses that have advertised very smartly for very little financial outlay.

Look realistically at what you can afford on a weekly basis, set this money aside and assess your marketing options. Try not to be stressed about the amount of money that you have available—spend the time and energy deciding what to do with it.

Don't be afraid of telling people what your budget is, especially if they are trying to sell you some form of advertising. Tell them what you can afford and ask them what they can do to promote your business with this amount of money. Every deal is negotiable. If they want your business badly enough they will offer you an incentive to do business with them.

Another point that is worth mentioning is that spending any money on marketing is a waste of time if you can't give your customers what they want and, more importantly, what they expect. I always ask business operators to look long and hard at their business before they start marketing to make sure that they can meet these expectations. After all, what is the point of spending money on getting new customers only to have them come to your business once and then leave in disgust.

I remember recently a themed restaurant opened up. They had fantastic pre-opening marketing and there was a very real air of anticipation that the place was going to be very good. When it finally did open the food was lousy and the theming ordinary so people didn't go back. I expect this business to close its doors in the near future. They sold people the promise of a fun experience but they couldn't come up with the goods.

This book suggests many free and low-cost ideas that will bring you business. First of all make sure that your business can do what you say it can, then commit to a weekly budget to market it.

Do you want to find new customers or keep existing ones?

To put it bluntly, it costs a lot more to find new customers than it does to keep old ones. Figures vary from industry to industry but it is estimated that finding new customers costs nine times as much as keeping existing customers.

The moral to this story is for you to have a good, honest look at your business and ask yourself the following questions:

1. Do you offer good service and value for money?
2. Do your customers keep coming back or do you see them once and never again?
3. Do you stay in touch with your customers after they have made a purchase?
4. Do you reward customers for being loyal to your business?

Complacency can be a big problem, especially for businesses that have been established for more than a few years. All industries are highly competitive and more than ever we all need to be smarter. One of the smartest business strategies is to look after your existing customers. Nurture them, encourage them to spend more with your business, continually ask them for ways to improve your current level of service and range of products. Stay in touch with your customers, reward them for being loyal and they will stay with you for many years.

The story of a Sydney cafe comes to mind. All regulars at this coffee shop have their own mug. They are quality mugs with the individual's name printed on the side and they all hang on hooks on an enormous wall. There are hundreds of them. Regulars walk into the coffee shop, grab their mug, take it to the counter and place their order—their preferred style of coffee is computerised and comes up as soon as the customer's name is entered. Mug holders are offered a variety of regular specials. In other words, they are made to feel very special. This is a very successful coffee shop. Many of the ideas recommended in this book focus on customer service. The extra revenue you're seeking may be closer than you think.

Do you have 'small business syndrome'?

I often meet small business operators who say that they can't do the type of marketing that big corporations do because they don't have anywhere near the same large budgets. I say why not? I call this the small business syndrome and I hear it all the time.

Big business spends a lot of money on advertising and marketing. Large corporations have to invest millions of dollars on market research and high profile advertising on television, radio and in newspapers just to maintain their share of the market. Competition is always strong and at the end of the day, the companies with the best marketing, backed up with good products and good service, tend to be the most successful.

How different is this for a small business? I believe that there is really no difference except for the number of zeros attached to the size of the budget. If an advertising or marketing idea works for a large company, why can't you, the small business operator, adopt the same idea?

A prime example of this is the customer loyalty program used by many large corporations. The most well known loyalty programs are the frequent flyer campaigns offered by virtually every airline around the world. The basic principle of this system is that the more you fly with one particular company (and its associated partner airlines) the more free flights and other bonuses you will receive.

Why can't this principle be used by any small business from a coffee shop to a car wash? Reward your customers for being loyal. By doing this you are acknowledging that your customers have a choice and they have chosen you.

The loyalty program is discussed in more detail later in this book and there are many other ideas used by big business that can easily be adapted and used by smaller businesses for a fraction of the cost.

Forget about the 'small business syndrome' and use the ideas that big corporations have proven to work; then reap the rewards of their investment. All of the ideas in this book are used by major corporations.

What is market research and do you need it?

Most people in business either ignore market research as something that only big companies can afford or, alternatively, they class it as one of those terms that people throw around without really understanding what it means.

Market research is one of the most powerful marketing tools for any business. Market research is basically asking either potential customers or existing customers (sometimes both) a few simple questions. The answers to these questions are then used to formulate the future of your business. Market research is a lot cheaper than going broke because of a bad decision.

For example, imagine that you run a bakery and you are thinking about adding a takeaway food outlet to the front of the factory. There are two ways that you can go about this. The first is to buy all of the new equipment, employ the staff, change the signage, advertise and then sit back and hope that the crowd breaks the door down. This is the way that the majority of business ideas tend to evolve; and for every one that works there are hundreds that fail.

The second way to go about this project is to do a bit of market research first. Formulate a few simple questions to ask your customers. For example:

1. Do you buy lunch from a takeaway restaurant?
2. How far do you have to travel?
3. Is the food good or do you shop there because it is convenient?
4. If we had a takeaway food outlet, would you consider trying us?
5. What type of food would you like to be able to buy for lunch?
6. What other items do you need on a regular basis that you think we should stock (for example, newspapers, magazines etc.)?
7. Would it be convenient for you if we were open late in the afternoon so that you could by pre-made meals to take home for dinner?

The next step is to start talking to everyone who could be a potential customer. Pay someone to go door-to-door or jump on the phone and start ringing potential customers.

Most people are quite happy to answer a survey as long as you quickly clarify who you are and what you want and emphasise that it will only take a few seconds. For example:

Hi, my name is Bob and I'm calling from Bob's Bakery. We are thinking of starting up a takeaway food business at the bakery and I was wondering if I could ask you a couple of quick questions?

I have conducted a lot of market research campaigns like this and the results are quite astonishing. People feel important because you have taken the time to ask them their opinion and, most importantly, you will receive valuable information about exactly what the market wants, not what you feel the market wants—two very different pieces of information.

Once the questionnaires have been completed you will need to interpret the information. You need to look for trends and majority answers. If 99 per cent of the responses said that they buy their lunch from 'Tom's Takeaway' and they have for a hundred years and, most importantly, they love it, you may have a problem. If they said that they use 'Tom's Takeaway' because it's close but the food is lousy and the staff are rude, you probably have a winner on your hands.

Another commonly used form of market research is the 'mystery shopper'. This is the practice of hiring someone to buy something from your business to assess how good your service is. There are companies established that do this. Our company does a lot of 'mystery shopper' and, like all market research, the results are always interesting.

Some of the items assessed include the appearance of your business, the promptness of the service, after-sales follow-up, technical knowledge, telephone manner, pricing etc. I recently conducted a campaign like this for a limousine company. They asked me to request rates and information on hiring a limousine for a wedding from their company and from their six main competitors. The results were amazing.

The survey results showed that they offered the best customer service but their pricing was confusing and they did not have a brochure to send out—two problems that they were aware of but the survey reinforced the urgency of sorting them out. Their six competitors were far worse. Each of the six promised to send out a brochure—not one did. None of the competitors even bothered to make a follow-up call.

My advice following the survey was simple—send out a brochure and make a follow-up call and they were 90 per cent more likely to get the business.

Market research can be as simple as asking someone how they heard about your business. This tells you if the marketing dollars you are spending are working. Hopefully a lot of your business comes from word-of-mouth recommendations from other satisfied customers, a topic that is talked about in greater detail later in the book.

A common problem with companies doing market research is that if they don't like the answers, they ignore them. If you are going to take the time, cost and effort to do market research be honest enough to listen to the results and to do something about them. The success of your business depends on knowing and understanding the needs of your current customers and the needs of your potential customers. Market research should be ongoing, targeting different aspects of your business on a regular basis.

Once again, of all the companies I have dealt with, those that are the most successful regularly conduct market research at all levels with their customers, their staff and even their competitors. They use the information that they collect to improve their level of service and to plan the future direction of their business.

What type of promotional material should you use?

Promotional material evolves as your business matures. Today it may be a simple, one-page, photocopied flyer that can be dropped into letterboxes if that is all that you can afford. Perhaps tomorrow you will have a glossy magazine featuring your offices around the world. The main aim is to always make the best promotional material that you can afford at the time. People will form an opinion of your company based on your promotional material. Successful businesses have good quality promotional material that they are proud to hand out.

Promotional material covers everything from business cards through to brochures, flyers, signage, uniforms and websites. The most common marketing weakness I have observed is that small businesses generally have very poor promotional material. Brochures are cluttered with masses of information, poor choices of colour and a complete lack of excitement. They are hard to read and they are boring.

It doesn't matter what your product is, more people will use it if it looks interesting and exciting and your company looks professional and secure.

There is a misconception that to produce flashy brochures costs a lot of money—it used to. Today there is a lot of technology around that has made producing promotional material a lot cheaper. If you don't know what you want, try to find samples of promotional material that you like and copy the format or the layout (beware of copyright laws that make it illegal to copy items exactly). Take the sample to a designer or desktop publisher and get them to style your promotional material around the sample that you have provided.

At the end of the day it costs the same amount of money to produce a lousy brochure as it does to produce a good one. Take the time, get the advice and make your promotional material the best quality that you can afford. Be proud to show people your flyers, business cards and brochures.

Another point to remember is the old saying that a picture is far better than a thousand words when it comes to selling products. Always use photographs where possible and try to make the pictures the best quality available. An example of this is portraits. It really is relatively inexpensive to have photographs taken in a studio and the results are fabulous. These photographs reproduced in your promotional material will look a thousand times better than the happy snap of you at the beach.

From my experience, good promotional material results in good sales. If you have poor promotional material, be big enough to change. I have seen many businesses that think nothing of spending $200 000 to set up their business but cringe at spending $2000 to produce a quality brochure.

Another important point to remember with promotional material is to make it stand out from the crowd and your opposition. Always compare brochures, look for new and innovative ideas that catch your attention and, most importantly, identify what makes you want to buy a particular product. If it worked on you, perhaps it will work on your potential customers.

Do you need a holiday before you get started?

Are you feeling dynamic and ready to leap into marketing or is this the last ditch effort at survival? A lot of small business operators come to me at the desperation stage, completely burnt out with their nerves on edge. My marketing advice to them is to have a holiday.

A positive attitude is the best weapon that any business owner or manager can have. Sometimes it is easier said than done. However, from my experience there are two distinct types of business people. The first type opens the doors and waits for the customers to start rolling in. They generally do not advertise, saying that it is a waste of time and money. The customers don't come through the door so they begin to get disgruntled and they become more and more negative as each day goes by. There are a hundred reasons why the business is not working and nothing is their fault—it's the economy or the guy up the road or the government. From my experience these businesses go broke—often.

The second type of business is run by positive and cheery people. They are well presented, friendly and open to ideas. They believe in trying different approaches to marketing and advertising. They understand that marketing is an essential part of their business. Their customers leave this business satisfied with their experience and, in all likelihood, they will return and tell lots of other people about their experience. These businesses tend to succeed.

It is not necessarily how much money you have in the bank or how much experience you have that determine the success of your business. A positive attitude and enthusiasm for what you are doing are two very powerful tools in the successful business person's armoury.

If you are fried how can you expect to get good results from marketing? Of course it is never a good time to have a holiday—either you are too busy or you haven't got any money or there is no one to look after the business when you are away.

A friend of mine runs an electrical appliance repair shop. This is a demanding business that regularly requires him to be called out to repair machines. He often complained about how trapped he felt in his business. An opportunity presented itself for him to go to Antarctica for ten weeks. As he was an avid photographer the opportunity was too good to pass up but he was deeply concerned that his customers wouldn't understand and he would lose his business. He went anyway, basically shutting the business for the time he was gone. In short, he had the trip of a lifetime and, a few weeks after arriving home, it was business as usual. He may have lost a few customers but he picked up new ones relatively quickly. The holiday did him the world of good and more than likely did his business the world of good because he came back refreshed and positive. The moral to this story is that there is never a good time to have a break but sometimes you shouldn't let that stop you.

How well do you know your competitors' businesses?

It is critically important to know exactly what products and services your competitors offer. How can you compete against a business if you don't know what you are competing against?

From my experience with small business, as soon as you ask any proprietor about competing businesses there are two general responses. The first is that they begin a scathing dialogue on how incompetent their competitors are, how expensive, how unreliable and so on. The second response is a surprised look reflecting the fact that they know absolutely nothing about their competitors.

A very important rule in running a successful business is to make certain that you and your staff never, ever, knock a competitor. If you are uncertain about the work that they provide say so, but never ridicule them or their products. Learn to sell your business on your qualities, not the opposition's shortfalls.

To find out information about your competitors is really quite easy. You can call the company directly, read through their advertisements, ask your friends and family if they have used this business and ask them how they found the service that they received. Once you are clear on what they offer you can promote your business around what makes you different and hopefully better, so that potential customers will buy from you.

Many businesses view competitors as the enemy when in reality they can be friends. Smart businesses working together can form a very strong alliance. For example, imagine two cleaning companies helping each other and working together. Imagine for a second that these two companies decide that if either is too busy to do a job when a customer calls they will recommend the other. If one runs short on cleaning chemicals out of hours the other will help out. They can agree on the boundaries and the clients that each company will target (be very careful when it comes to pricing as it is illegal to fix prices in many countries).

If you are lucky enough to be able to work with your competition, that is fantastic. If not, at least make a point of knowing and understanding what the competition offers so that you can offer more.

Have you had bad experiences with marketing in the past?

I often hear business operators saying that they tried this or they tried that and it didn't work. They then make amazing statements such as television advertising is a waste of money or newspaper advertising doesn't work. I try to suggest that there are a lot of factors that make marketing work and you need to have as many of them on your side as possible to get results.

I remember several years ago a friend of mine who runs a prominent tourist attraction ran a Mother's Day special offer in the newspaper. The advertisement said that all mothers could have free admission on Mother's Day. The newspaper made a mistake and doubled the size of the advertisement. The result was amazing and the attraction had their busiest day on record.

The following year they ran the same advertisement again at the larger size thinking that it was the size of the advertisement that had produced these amazing results. This time they had a shocking day. Why?

On the previous Mother's Day it was pouring with rain and this attraction was undercover. The weather on the latest Mother's Day was sensational so everyone was outdoors. Add to this a huge festival that coincidentally ran on the same day and what was a successful promotion the year before turned into a disaster the year after.

The point that I am trying to make is that there is absolutely no doubt that traditional advertising mediums, like television, radio and newspaper, work. If they didn't work for some promotion that you did in the past try to identify why. That is the key to the problem. Remove what didn't work and try it again. Once you get it right don't change the formula until it stops working.

Another interesting point that I have observed is that people's expectations of the business they will generate from advertising is often unrealistic. I meet people who think that a $50 advertisement will bring in $50 000. If it did, every business would be successful. The fact is that there are no magic formulas to tell you how much business you should expect when you place an advertisement. If you can cover the cost of the advertisement you are in front—everything else is a bonus.

Successful marketing is a matter of persistence to get the formula right.

What is a successful business?

There are many ways to gauge the success of a business. Unfortunately many of them are based purely on monetary measures. I encounter a lot of business operators who are extremely hard on themselves. Because their business may be going through a tough time they blame themselves and start to develop the feeling that they are failures at what they do.

I would like to take this opportunity to have my say on what makes a business successful.

First, the fact that a person is prepared to move out of the comfort zone to take a risk and put their own neck on the financial chopping block makes them a success. Having a weekly pay packet would be the greatest feeling for most business operators who tend to struggle from day to day. I remember when I started my first business. I was 18 years old and I had times when I didn't have enough money to put petrol in the car to get home so I slept in the shop—sometimes for a week at a time. I am not trying to be a martyr but I am showing the degree of dedication that many business operators have.

Second, I am constantly impressed by the quality of service and the products produced by small business. I am certain that some people must think that small, one-person companies couldn't possibly make any products or offer any services of world-class quality. I disagree completely and I see evidence of this fact every day. There are some incredibly talented and dedicated people out there who are striving for excellence in ways that the world's largest corporations could never imagine.

Finally, the degree of perseverance that I see from many small business operators constantly amazes me. I have had people come to me who have lost everything at the age of 60 and they want some marketing advice on their next venture. They smile, they are positive and they are wise.

Small business operators are often embarrassed to say that they are having financial difficulties. I try to explain that there wouldn't be a business in the world that hasn't experienced cash flow problems at some time or another so don't beat yourself up because you are having a tough time.

There are many other ways to measure success apart from purely monetary results. Success is achieved by having great products, offering exceptional service, having a strong rapport with your staff and knowing within yourself that you have done a good job.

Ten important tips for running a successful business

The following points are based on my observations of successful business operators. I believe that they are all equally important.

1. Surround yourself with positive people and keep negativity out of your life. If you don't like what you are doing then start planning to change the business you are in. It is amazing how much money you can make when you love what you do.
2. If you promise to do something, then make sure that you do it. One of the biggest downfalls of small businesses is a lack of reliability. The biggest compliment I can get from a client is when they commend me for doing a job on time and on budget.
3. Be organised. Take the time to organise those records, balance the cheque book and clear the desk or tidy the workshop. Working in a cluttered environment invites mistakes and inefficiency.
4. Take pride in your appearance. Iron those overalls, tidy the office and put some flowers in the waiting room—people notice. If you look good you will feel good and your business will benefit.
5. Compliment people sincerely—your family, your staff and your customers. If you haven't got anything nice to say, sell up and move away.
6. Treat everyone that walks in the door as a potential customer—even if they are trying to sell you something, one day they may be looking to buy something as well.

7. Don't worry about lack of money—work on making money. Worrying about a bill never got it paid any faster. Spend the time implementing some simple marketing ideas and figuring out how to get more customers in the door.

8. Be open to new and innovative ideas. If you find yourself saying the dreaded words, 'that's the way we have always done it and that's the way we are going to keep doing it', perhaps you are not as flexible and open as you could be. An idea that could make you a lot of money may be in the head of a friend or staff member who feels that you would not be receptive if they voiced their suggestion. Encourage innovative and open thinking.

9. Be completely honest and ethical in every dealing that you have. It is important that you are able to walk down the street with your head held high.

10. Take time out to relax and recharge your batteries. You don't get a medal if you work non-stop for ten years— you get hardened arteries, ulcers and a sore back. It's not about money, it's about taking time for you. It is a time to eat well, catch up with the friends that you are always too busy to see, throw the dog a Frisbee, see a movie, go fishing or just catch up on missed sleep.

2 | Does your business stand out from the crowd?

Standing out from the crowd is important and it really is one of the main fundamentals of any marketing strategy. These days people have a lot of choice. With the advent of the Internet that choice has increased even more. If people can't find your number easily or if you are hidden away among your competitors you may be in trouble. It is important to send out a very clear message that you are here, you are ready, willing and able to be of service and most importantly of all that you are great at what you do. There are various ways to increase your chances of standing out from the crowd and these ideas are detailed in this section:

#1   Promote your business from the outside in
#2   Put your message on the company car
#3   Turn your invoice into a sales tool
#4   Sell yourself even when you're not there
#5   Use the Internet to be noticed
#6   A good uniform impresses everyone
#7   Make the most of packaging
#8   Never underestimate the importance of a business card
#9   Does your business have a memorable name?

1 Promote your business from the outside in

Be proud to promote your business by putting a sign on the wall. I used to deal with a large graphic design company that had an upstairs office on one of the busiest intersections in town. They had a huge wall in full view from anywhere on the intersection and they never got around to painting a sign on this wall. Eventually they moved out because business was bad. If they had spent a few hundred dollars on a simple sign business would have got a whole lot better a whole lot faster.

Outdoor signage works seven days a week, 24 hours a day, whether you are open or closed. Use it to its full advantage. Be aware of local government regulations governing signage restrictions such as size. Work with these regulations but make your signs as big as you legally can. Don't clutter them, just a few words outlining what you do and when you are open. Make the colours stand out and check any artwork thoroughly for spelling or grammatical mistakes.

I once had a SCUBA Diving School. One day I put a dummy on the roof dressed in old diving equipment and it looked real. The amount of coverage and exposure that this dummy gave my business was quite extraordinary—to the point that one night it was stolen. The local radio, television and newspaper all took the story on and a great hunt began to find the dummy. I later estimated that this dummy and the loss of it gave my business approximately $20 000 worth of free advertising.

Before you decide on sign-writing, drive around and look at other businesses to see what styles you like and what catches your eye. Visit your competitors' offices, shops or factories to determine how you could make your business signage more appealing to potential customers.

Remember to make your sign-writing match your corporate image and company colours, otherwise things can start to become messy and confusing to your potential customers. Keep all sign-writing simple and easy to read. The new saying that 'less is more' definitely applies to sign-writing.

By the way, when you plan your sign-writing remember to include what days you are open or what your trading hours are. There is nothing worse than sitting outside a business at 8.15 a.m. on a Saturday morning, wondering if it will open at all that day or if it will open at 8.30 a.m. or 9.00 a.m.

2 Put your message on the company car

Like all outdoor signage, company vehicles are an excellent way to promote your business. Most businesses have at least one company vehicle that can be anything from a utility to a bus. These vehicles tend to be on the road all day, all over the city. What better way to tell people about your business than a moving sign?

Sign-writing on vehicles can be expensive; however, like all advertising, do it to suit your budget. Perhaps start with a set of magnetic signs for the doors and then work your way up to a full paint job.

There are a few key points to remember with any form of moving advertising—keep words to a minimum, make it easy to read and tell people where they can find you and when you are open.

Many companies have overcome this by putting the Yellow Pages sticker on their vehicle. This works well as long as your company is easy to find in the Yellow Pages. If it isn't it should be. Don't make it hard for customers to find you.

A few words of warning with sign-writing on vehicles— you get what you pay for so make sure that the sign-writer gives you a few samples of the work that they have done previously before committing yourself.

I used to have a business partner who was probably the world's worst driver. He was fast, aggressive and all over the road. This was bad enough in his car but when he was in the company vehicle I would receive phone call after phone call from angry motorists abusing me because of the way this maniac was driving. Every time my partner took the car on the road we lost customers. The point here is to make certain that anyone driving your company vehicle is aware that if your name is on the side they are representing your business and should drive safely and courteously.

If the people driving your company vehicle are responsible, don't hesitate to plaster the car with signs telling the world all about your business and the products and services that you offer.

Other clever ideas are the cliché ideas like the large telephone on top of the pizza delivery vehicles. One company that sells exhaust fans has a fan fitted on top of all of its service vehicles, which does look very impressive. The giant cockroach is a favourite of pest control companies.

If you put some thought into what your company does the results can be visually stunning. Imagine a pet shop with a giant dog bone on top of the car or a mechanic with a giant spanner on the roof, perhaps a giant baby on top of the baby equipment hire company vehicle.

Sign-writing company vehicles is a great idea. Your sign-writing will promote your business all day, every day.

3 Turn your invoice into a sales tool

Most companies send out invoices and statements on a regular basis. Invoices are normally passed through a number of hands before they actually reach the person that signs the cheque. This provides the opportunity for you to promote your business to a number of people who are already aware of what you basically do but perhaps not of every facet of what your business has to offer.

This is what we call a 'soft sell' or 'positive reinforcement' of your company message. Perhaps you are going to stock a new range or product, perhaps pricing has changed, or your trading hours are different or you simply want to reinforce the strong corporate message that you are already putting across.

A computer software company I dealt with used their company invoice to introduce a new member of staff every month. For example, January's invoice had a picture of Bill Higgins, Sales Manager, with a brief outline of his career history and what role he played in the company. This gave a very personal feel to their business and increased my level of awareness regarding the people that I was dealing with.

The introduction of a company staff member also took the emphasis off the invoice being a bill and I am sure that I paid these accounts much quicker because they had a very personal feel to them. I also felt as if I was a part of that company, a valued customer being shown the inner workings of a successful business.

Another company that I used to deal with always sent out a flyer with jokes, positive affirmations, motivational passages and generally interesting material. It was always a joy to get these invoices and I know that these ones were paid early. They put a smile on my face so I believed that they deserved to be paid quickly. How many bills do you look forward to receiving?

I have also heard of this method being used when

people are late paying their invoices. Put a picture of your family in the envelope with a quick note on the back saying that it is 'hard to feed our children when your company is slow paying their bill'. This is very effective. Of course you may need to pick your customer as this may not be appropriate for some. This idea can of course be made quite humorous depending on how you do it, perhaps sending a photograph of your dog looking sadly at an empty dinner bowl or an empty cookie jar or something similar.

Another effective way to get people to notice and to read your invoices is to use really bright colours. Our invoices are sent on fluorescent green paper that almost glows in the dark. It is always an icebreaker if we are chasing an overdue account as everyone remembers the infamous lime green invoice.

Invoices can become powerful marketing tools and, really, the very worst that can happen is that you get paid faster. As you are already sending out invoices the only extra cost is in the production of the flyer.

4 Sell yourself even when you're not there

Everybody hates being put on hold but unfortunately it is a way of life. If you have the technology to play hold music you can probably arrange to have a company message playing. This is an opportune time to let potential customers know more about your company and the services that you offer.

There are plenty of companies that arrange 'messages on hold' and the cost is not overly expensive. Like most of these marketing ideas it is more a matter of someone making the time to find the company that produces 'messages on hold' and then actually arranging for the service to be installed. This type of marketing produces a very good corporate image and many small companies give the appearance of being a large company by having a professional on hold message.

The same principle can apply with answering machines and voice mail on mobile phones. Be proud of your business and take every opportunity to promote your services. Try the following:

> *Instead of*
> 'Hi, you've reached Jim Davies. I can't take your call at the moment but please leave your name and number and I'll call you back as soon as possible.'
> *try this*
> 'Hi, you've reached Jim Davies of Precision Engine Tuning, the mechanical repair specialist in Brooklyn.
> I can't take your call at the moment but I would love the opportunity to return your call and discuss how Precision Engine Tuning can be of service to you.'

Keep your message brief and to the point, taking advantage of the fact that people are calling you but being courteous to the fact that people are busy and they don't want to spend ten minutes sitting on the phone listening to the virtues of your company. It doesn't cost you a cent to leave a more detailed message and if you get one extra client per year it was worth the effort.

I did make an interesting call recently to a large finance company. As usual there were a hundred choices to make, press this and then press that and finally a breath of fresh air. The prompt came, 'If you are sick of waiting and sick of choices press 9', which I did and they had a recording playing of a comedian who was making fun of telephone on hold systems, which gave me a laugh while I waited for one of their customer service staff to answer my call.

5 Use the Internet to be noticed

The Internet is a new and exciting resource that has enormous potential. Advertising on the Internet is a new concept that many businesses don't really understand. I personally look at the Internet like a big library. You know that all of the information is there; it's just a matter of finding it. The amount of information available is virtually beyond comprehension but the key to success is making it easy for people to find your business or product.

Basically there are two ways to promote your business on the Internet. The first is that you can have your own website where people surfing the net may come across your site and decide that they want more information or that they would like to purchase what you are selling. Setting up your own site is becoming cheaper every day and within a couple of years the majority of businesses will have their own websites. Websites can easily be linked to other sites, making it easier for you to be found.

There are companies available that sell fully designed and very impressive websites that you purchase. They simply fill in the blanks and put your company name and your products and services in the right place. So for a few hundred dollars you can have a very professional website up and running. To find these companies search for 'website hosting, web design and domain names' on the Internet. Many of the companies that offer this service advertise heavily on search engine sites.

The second way to promote your business on the Internet is to purchase what are known as banner advertisements. This is where you put an advertisement on someone else's website. The advantage of this is simply that you can promote your business on a highly successful site that is established and perhaps getting hundreds of thousands of 'hits' per month.

To emphasise this point, imagine you have written a

book on *Alien Abductions* and you have decided that the Internet is the medium to promote and sell the book. For about three hundred dollars you could set up a website with a basic layout and sit back and hope that people find you.

The alternative is to spend a few thousand dollars and take a banner advertisement at an established UFO site—one that has up to 70 000 'hits' or visits per day. The advertisement will cost a lot of money but you have access to a huge number of people that have already shown an interest in the subject that you have written about.

The Internet is an amazing tool with unlimited potential. While I was having a quick swim on the Internet recently I came across a fruit and vegetable store that home delivers their produce throughout the city. You email them your order and it is delivered the same day. They have a virtual grocery store on the Net and you simply look through the produce and make your purchases by credit card.

I was at a seminar recently when the host explained how his American-based company purchased their letterhead and business cards from a printer in Malaysia via the Internet. They used to buy their stationery from the printer next door to them but they found that the goods they ordered from Malaysia arrived quicker and were less expensive.

Now the competition is not the shop up the road but all of the shops around the world. Don't be scared of the Internet—use it to your advantage. Remember to include your email address or website on all of your promotional material and in any advertisement.

6 A good uniform impresses everyone

An interesting phenomenon happens when you put a person in a uniform—generally they are treated with more respect because it looks like they have some form of authority. This is one of the main reasons why the military and the police dress in uniforms.

Imagine if an airline pilot strolled through the cabin in a Disneyland T-shirt and shorts—how much confidence would this instil in passengers? I would hazard a guess and say not much. In fact, if I was on that particular flight I would be out the door in a second.

If you and your staff are not well presented in smart and practical uniforms maybe you are not sending the right message to your customers. Uniforms tend to be costly but, like most marketing tools, you purchase them to suit your budget. Perhaps you can start with matching shirts and name tags and work up to skirts, trousers and shorts. Quite often staff will be prepared to pay some of the costs towards their uniforms because it saves them the problem and expense of continually buying new clothes for work.

Once again, find a company uniform that you like and see if you can apply it to your business. Even very small businesses can have a uniform—the size of the business is irrelevant. Once a uniform is established make certain that everyone is clear about how they are expected to wear it. The better presented you and your staff appear the more professional your business will appear. This will instil confidence and security in customers when they use your services.

There are shops that specialise in selling uniforms and accessories. They can be found in the Yellow Pages telephone directory.

Even if you feel that you don't require uniforms or you can't afford them, make sure that you and your staff are always dressed neatly with clean, ironed clothes.

7 Make the most of packaging

Many businesses provide packaging for their products. This may be something as simple as a cheap plastic bag right through to an enormous wooden crate. Packaging provides the perfect opportunity for a company message to be passed on to potential customers that see the packaging as well as to the customer receiving the package. If you are providing the packaging anyway why not use it to increase your sales. Print a company slogan on your wrapping paper, perhaps your trading hours, gift suggestions, new products, change of address information or any other message that you can think of.

Another easy idea that is very rarely used is to slip in a promotional flyer when packaging up an item. If a person has bought something from your business there is a good chance that they will buy something else in the future or perhaps recommend you to a friend.

Book stores are one of the few industries that really take advantage of the potential of in-packaging promotions. Most will include a flyer covering specials of the month, latest releases and special interest type publications as well as giving you a free bookmark promoting a latest release.

I heard about an idea in Japan where a major shopping centre in Tokyo has a city map printed on their bags. People all over town run around finding their way through the hustle and bustle with this detailed map, which of course also promotes the centre as the best place to shop in Tokyo.

8 Never underestimate the importance of a business card

Business cards are often considered a necessary evil rather than a fantastic marketing tool. Potential customers deduce a lot from your appearance and that of your business card. Make the effort and use your business card to its full potential.

Business cards are normally printed in sheets, which means that you can have a number of different messages or names. By all means use some for names but use the others as mini brochures. Putting your services on the backof a business card only adds marginally to the production cost but it enhances your card and makes it a very effective tool.

Another option is to have 'bring this card in and receive the following . . .' on your business card. Coffee shops seem to have adopted this idea on mass with virtually every cafe offering a coffee card where you pay for so many cups and you get one free. The business card is your progress record, which is crossed off each time you make a purchase.

This concept works well with restaurants that offer either a free glass of wine with a meal or a free dessert with dinner. The offer is printed on the back of the card and to redeem it the customer must produce the card when dining.

There are many businesses that could use this concept to easily increase the amount of business they are receiving from both new and existing customers.

Once you have fully utilised your business cards the next important step is to distribute them everywhere. The price difference between printing 2000 and 3000 business cards is, once again, quite small—the more you print, the cheaper they become. Put them on noticeboards, in letterboxes, in a stand on your counter, give them to your suppliers, mail them out or stand on a street corner handing them out.

People save business cards. If yours looks good and it

has more information about your company than just the business name you can bet that people will hang on to it. One way to encourage people to hang on to your business card is to make it a phone card. Companies that specialise in making phone cards are often more than willing to do a deal where you buy a certain number of phone cards from them and they will print your company message on the front. They may even offer a few dollars in free calls in the hope that the person receiving the card will recharge it once the initial credit is used.

Any unusual business card ideas will generally be good for attracting attention. I have seen some great musical business cards, scented business cards and even glow in the dark business cards. Look at printing business cards as an opportunity, not as a chore. Have some fun and try to come up with an unusual idea that will make people sit up and take notice of your business simply because you have developed an unusual business card.

9 Does your business have a memorable name?

Having a good business name is a very important factor in standing out from the crowd. I get very frustrated when I see businesses with names that really don't seem to make sense to me. Sometimes I think people try to be too clever when it comes to naming a business.

If you have a million dollars to promote your business name you can saturate television and newspapers to educate the general public. If you have a limited marketing budget your name becomes another marketing tool, not a marketing liability. By all means choose a name that is different and funny but try to tell people what you do.

Everyone will want to give you their opinion when it comes to choosing a name. How do you decide what is right and what is wrong? There is probably no right or wrong but there are a few points that can increase the effectiveness of your name. Try some of these:

1. Try to include what your business does in your name.
    Real Estate
2. You can include your name to give the business a more personal feel.
    Roger's Real Estate
3. Include your location if you plan to focus on one area.
    Roger's Russian Real Estate
4. If you specialise try to put that in your name as well.
    Roger's Russian Residential Real Estate

Our business name used to be 'Australian Business and Marketing Solutions'. People had fallen asleep by the time they were half way through it. We became known as 'Solutions Marketing' which suited us as it said what we do in a fairly simple way. As our business grew and we began to take on more corporate and government work we changed our company name to 'The Marketing Professionals' to reflect a new image and a level of professionalism that we were aspiring to.

The point to this is that business names can change and it isn't the end of the world. While I am not an advocate for changing your name once a week, I do believe that if you have a poor business name that is confusing you should change it. Business names evolve and what you were called five years ago may no longer be relevant for what you do today.

I often laugh when I remember coming across a bakery in the middle of America that was called something like Randy's Auto Repairs. I found it intriguing so I had to go inside and ask why. Randy told me that he was a lousy mechanic but a great pie maker. Over the years people stopped coming to him for mechanical work and started coming for his peach pies (which were simply sensational I might add) so he decided to do what he did best.

Decide what type of message you would like to give your customers and then decide on a name to suit that image. Don't be afraid of changing your business name if the focus of the work you offer or the products that you produce have changed.

3 | Do you make the most of the customers you already have?

It is cheaper to keep existing customers than it is to find new ones. Successful businesses work very hard at building solid relationships with their customers. They reward them for shopping regularly, they ask for feedback, they look for ways to constantly improve both the products and the services they are offering. They also never take their customers for granted. The best way to look after existing customers is to stay in touch with them. If you haven't done this in the past, don't worry, it is never too late to send someone a letter to say thank you for their business. The ideas we'll talk about in this section are:

#10   Send out reminder notices
#11   Stay in touch with your customers
#12   Remember important dates
#13   Ask your customers for referrals
#14   Say thank you to generate more business
#15   What is a loyalty program and can you use one?

10 Send out reminder notices

This marketing initiative seems to have only been utilised by dentists, optometrists, the blood bank and vets. Whenever you (or your pets) are due for a check-up you receive a gentle reminder in the mail. What a great idea.

So why doesn't your mechanic send out reminder notices—'Hey, it's been six months since your last service, you better bring the car in'. Or perhaps your solicitor—'It's been two years since we have seen you, perhaps it's time to make a new will'.

This type of mail-out or phone call can bring great results and really all it takes is for you to have records of your clients. It is a gentle, no pressure reminder and a call to action. One dentist I know even goes so far as to schedule an appointment for the clients, letting them know that they will be in touch to confirm the appointment one week prior.

Imagine if every six months a letter turned up smelling of perfume. Out of curiosity you open it and inside is a scented Christmas tree—the type that deodorise your car. Attached is a brief note from your mechanic saying, 'It's been six months since we saw you so your Christmas tree probably needs changing—just like your oil. Joe from our service department will call you in a few days to see if you would like to arrange a convenient time for a service.' One Christmas tree deodoriser and postage will come to about $3.50. I have never had a car serviced for under $100 (normally double this amount), so for a $3.50 investment you are probably going to make a $100 sale—sounds like good business to me.

A stationery company that I buy laser printer refills from knows that I use a cartridge every three to four weeks. Without fail I get a phone call during the third week of the month, asking me if I need another cartridge. I find this very convenient and I am never faced with the dilemma of running out of toner on a Saturday afternoon when I am in the middle of printing out a 300 page document.

Deep down I also like the fact that this company considers me important enough to track my consumer habits. It is also one less thing for me to worry about on a day-to-day basis.

11 Stay in touch with your customers

I was recently approached by a small aluminium manufacturing company. They were having a difficult time as
their particular industry had become very competitive in
the last few years. After a few minutes of discussing what
the main problem was (not enough customers) I asked how
long had they been in business. My jaw dropped when they
said almost twenty years and during that time they had
almost 20 000 customers.

After probing for a few more details it became apparent
that once a job was finished and delivered this business had
no further contact with the customer. There was no follow-
up or after-sales service. Sitting on the floor in some dusty
corner was a box filled with the names of thousands of
customers that had already used this business but had never
been followed up. This is a very common fault of small
business operators. They don't stay in touch with their past
customers because they don't know what to say.

The main product that the company offered was the
selling and installation of garage doors. To me it appeared
logical that they should offer a free after-sales service call
where they visit the house to oil the door, tension the chain
and generally make sure that everything is working well.
This provides two opportunities. First, the customer feels
good because the level of service they have received is great
and they will tell their friends. The second opportunity is
that the service person representing the company can cas-
ually outline the other services and products available,
hopefully making another sale.

If you have boxes of past client files laying in a dusty
corner, dig them out and get to work immediately. First of
all start communication with them. Drop them a line and
ask how your product is holding up. Let them know that
you will be sending updates about new and exciting products and services in the future. These people have already

walked through your door once. Assuming they were happy with your business, what is going to stop them from coming back again? Organise the records, check the addresses, phone numbers etc. and make sure that they are up to date and then get started.

Your best source of business could be tucked away in the garden shed under a stack of *National Geographic* magazines and old tax records.

12 Remember important dates

You can show your existing customers that you are interested in them by remembering important dates such as birthdays and anniversaries. This is the perfect opportunity for you to drop them a line to say congratulations and thank them for their business.

Find out your customers' birthdays by doing a brief survey. If you have a club of some sort make this information part of the sign-up form. Send the customer a birthday card and make them a special offer to say thank you for their business.

Customers in this instance can be anyone from regular clientele right through to the chief executive officer at a company that you supply. Take the time to handwrite the card. Don't make it look mass produced. Be genuine in your comments but not overly personal if you don't know the person very well.

I remember visiting my local video shop and as I was hiring my choice the computer made a funny sound. The lady serving me looked up and wished me 'a Happy Birthday'. Further to this she told me that I could have any two videos free of charge as well as an ice-cream to celebrate my special day. I was very impressed with this service and the fact that I felt special. If you operate a computer-based business like this, it is easy to have the computer alert you to a person's birthday.

Why make it just birthdays? Why not a thank you card because it has been twelve months since a customer started using your business. I often wonder why marriage celebrants don't send out anniversary cards. What a great way to generate new business.

How many birthday cards do you get from your suppliers or businesses where you are a customer? Be different and, most importantly, be remembered. Attention to small details can be a major key to success.

13 Ask your customers for referrals

Referrals are simply when you ask an existing customer for the name of someone who they know who may be able to use your services or products. The main idea of a referral is that you contact the person being referred and tell them that your customer recommended that you call them.

It is the same as having someone on the inside. By mentioning the friend's or customer's name as a recommendation you automatically have your foot in the door. Referrals are a great way to generate new business.

Establishing a system where your current clients can provide you with the name of a friend or colleague who may be interested in your product or service is a very inexpensive way to generate extra business. It is a good idea to offer some form of reward for customers who offer referrals, such as a free product or a free service.

Many quality businesses receive a large proportion of their business from customer referrals. It is important that you feel confident enough to ask your customers for referrals—if they are happy with the work that you have done why wouldn't they be happy to pass on a lead to a new customer? You may be surprised at how willing people are to help you promote your business.

As a normal business practice it is a good idea to talk to the customer after all work is completed to make certain that they are 100 per cent satisfied. This is the perfect time to ask for the referral and also to really make certain that they are completely happy with the work that you have done.

Always be up-front and honest. I have often told my customers when I am going through a quiet time and I need some more work. All of a sudden I have a team of sales reps chasing business for me. I always find this very humbling and ring to say thank you for their help. There are a lot of cynical people in the world but I do believe that the majority of people will go out of their way to help others. In return for this I will always give 100 per cent for people who helped me in the past.

Don't be afraid to ask your customers to suggest some referrals for your business.

14 Say thank you to generate more business

A point that I have emphasised in this book is the importance of telling customers that you appreciate them. A very easy way to do this is to send your customers a 'thank you' certificate.

For a number of years I worked as a sales manager for a cruise ship company. Part of my job was to call on travel wholesalers in Asia and America. Any business we received was a bonus because we were starting from scratch. Our management were very appreciative of the confidence that these companies were showing in us by sending their customers on our vessels.

To say 'thank you' a series of plaques was developed and sent to the various companies as they reached certain targets. We sent a thank you certificate for their first booking and as the business grew the plaques became less frequent but more valuable.

I used to wonder if these large corporations really cared about getting a little plaque from a small operator like us on the other side of the globe. As time progressed and I called regularly on about 100 companies, I noticed that virtually all of them displayed their plaques and certificates with honour, normally in their waiting rooms or in their boardrooms. That's when it struck me that everyone loves to be appreciated.

It also struck me that our business received great exposure by being in a place of honour on the wall of a large travel company. The same wall where many of their customers come to book cruises.

Every business has customers that spend a lot and those that spend a little. Work out a budget to suit your business and make up some form of thank you certificate. It may be something as simple as a letter to the company or it may be an unusual plaque that represents the type of business you operate.

I once received a thank you gift from an accountant. It was a calculator with really big buttons. The firm's name was on the calculator with a message saying 'We appreciate your business'. The accompanying letter explained that, like the 'easy-to-use' calculator, they wanted to provide a service to my business that was 'easy to use'. I thought that this was very clever and I have remembered it for years.

We recently conducted a large survey of departing tourists at an international airport. It was a complicated project that involved a lot of communicating between our business and the airport management. The representative from the airport was very professional and helpful. This lady's assistance made the project run smoothly and successfully.

After the project was completed we sent a bunch of flowers and note expressing our sincere gratitude for the assistance that we had received.

This is something we always do. If someone goes out of their way to help us we like to go out of our way to thank them. Often we will send a letter to their boss explaining how a particular person went above and beyond the call of duty to assist us with a particular project.

We are always sincere in our praise and we only do it if the person has really been helpful. What we have found is that whenever we deal with the same person again they always go out of their way to help. We also generate a lot of business by doing this because the person that we have said thank you to tells everyone that we are a great company to deal with. Everyone wins.

Saying 'thank you' can take many different shapes. We recently purchased $200 dollars worth of damper for a promotion we were running. To say 'thank you' the baker gave us a huge loaf of crusty Italian bread. Now this was only a small gift on their behalf but we appreciated it and remembered their gesture enough to write about it in this book. Now we buy all of our bread from this baker.

You decide how best to thank your customers and business associates. They will take notice and you will benefit with extra business and word-of-mouth advertising that costs very little.

How many handwritten thank you notes do you receive in the post every day? If your letterbox is like mine I would guess that the answer is zero. People don't write thank you notes, but they should.

Buy some stamps, a bundle of postcards or greeting cards from the local newsagency and start writing. The response is instant and somewhat overwhelming. Showing that you appreciate your customers and their business is an important step in keeping the business for a long time.

One of the most successful car salespeople in the United States used to spend more on cards and postage every year than most of his colleagues earned. He used to sell between five and six vehicles every day of the week and most of his customers spent their lives buying cars from him. He sent birthday cards, thank you cards, Christmas cards, the lot. What he ended up with was a loyal client base that were his friends as well as his customers.

Who should you send a thank you card or note to? The answer is everyone.

15 What is a loyalty program and can you use one?

In simple terms a loyalty program is a structured way of giving a benefit to customers who use your business regularly. The aim is to make the rewards appealing enough so the customers will not use the opposition because they are trying to achieve some type of prize you are offering. The most famous loyalty programs are the ones run by the airlines—frequent flier campaigns. This does not mean they only work for large companies. In fact, I believe that they work far better for smaller companies if they are done properly.

I recently established a loyalty program for a children's after-school maths and English tutoring business, for under $50. The same principles were adopted as those used by large airlines and financial institutions, namely a reward for being a loyal customer and an incentive to tell your friends about the company.

This business had about 100 children attending classes on a weekly basis. The cost for tutoring in two subjects amounted to $20 per month per student. As with many small businesses, the lady operating this one started with minimal capital and no marketing expertise but she managed to build it up to a good size. However, it was proving difficult to break the 100 student barrier and get into her profit-making zone.

After taking a close look at the business and considering that the budget for marketing was very minimal, the best source of potential customers seemed to be with the existing parents. Based on 100 students it was fair to assume that this provided a pool of about 175 parents (taking into account single-parent families and multiple children in the one family).

A flyer was made on the company PC introducing the loyalty program. Basically, as students reached a milestone, such as three months, six months or twelve months, they received one month's free tutoring—the children probably did not care less about this but the parents did and they were the ones that signed the cheques.

Further to this the parents were given certificates to give to their friends and colleagues offering free academic testing for children. This initiative was used to encourage the friend or colleague to take their child along and be tested to assess their current academic level. If they decided to sign their children up for some coaching the referring parent received a free month's tuition for their own child. Smart parents found plenty of friends and received up to a year of free tutoring simply by referring other people to the coaching company in an easy and clear way.

This principle can be applied to virtually every business. If you have customers staying with you for a long time, reward them—they are your best form of advertising. Taking customers for granted is one of the greatest business tragedies.

Loyalty programs and incentives work exceptionally well. Take your time, plan it properly and follow it through. Talk to your customers about your idea; they will tell you what will motivate them to spend more with your business.

Many businesses, particularly restaurants, offer loyalty cards where regular customers receive a 10 per cent discount. Every time my wife and I go to our local Chinese restaurant, the owner, Mr Wong, hands us the bill with a 10 per cent discount. I always tell him that he doesn't have to do this but he insists. He states that we eat at his restaurant once per week and we tell lots of our friends how good his food is. He laughs and says that we generate half of his business making it well worth his 10 per cent discount.

Another idea I discovered and thought was very clever was with a local commercial cleaning company. Every year they offered to clean the houses of five staff members from their largest customers. These customers awarded the house cleaning as a prize for their staff members and basically everyone was happy. The cleaners had cemented their relationship with their clients. The clients had rewarded a few members of their team with a thank you prize and the staff members themselves had clean houses.

All businesses can benefit from rewarding customers for being loyal. The hard part is to determine how you can best reward your particular customers.

4 | How do you generate free 'word-of-mouth' advertising?

Word-of-mouth advertising is simply people telling other people about your business. There are two reasons that it is wonderful. The first is because it is free and the second is because it is believable. Generating word-of-mouth advertising is one of the best forms of marketing for companies with limited budgets because all you need to get it happening is time. This section looks at some of the easiest ways to generate free word-of-mouth advertising for your business:

#16   Writing a press release
#17   Everyone loves a winner
#18   Call the local radio station
#19   Ask your customers to tell their friends about you

16 Writing a press release

A press release is basically a facsimile sent to the media advising them of a special event or a newsworthy event they may be interested in covering. As part of the responsibility of being a marketing company we send out press releases for our customers all the time. We send these press releases to the television stations, newspapers, radio stations and industry publications if applicable.

Press releases are not just reserved for calamities and world shattering news. Quite often newspapers, radio and even television stations are very happy to release a story about a new product or major event. The main criterion is that it should not be blatant advertising but more a general interest story that helps to get your company name in the public profile.

It is worth remembering that the media need stories of interest and they are always looking for articles or stories that may appeal to their viewers.

Subjects that you could make a press release about include the following:

- a company milestone (ten years, 100 employees, new building etc.);
- an award of some sort;
- recognition from industry peers for an achievement;
- being successful in winning a contract;
- doing something that no one has done before;
- having a celebrity visit your business;
- a charity sponsorship; and
- an event that you are involved in.

Press releases should be short (a maximum of 250 words) with copies of relevant brochures and information to back up what you are saying. Where possible it is good to send out your press release several days before the actual event (if there is an event) to allow the various media agencies time to plan for the story.

Some of the specific information that you should include in your press release is:

- When did it happen?
- Who does it involve?
- What is the significance?
- Who is the best person to contact for comments (include their direct telephone number)?
- Where is the best place (and the best time) for a photo opportunity?

There is a sample of a press release in the Appendix at the back of this book. Feel free to copy this layout for your own press releases. Whenever the opportunity arises, take a few minutes and drop the local media a press release about your business.

17 Everyone loves a winner

If you take the time to enter awards for your particular industry you may actually win. Award-winning companies can advertise the fact and, without a doubt, your business will receive a lift in profile. Consumers will feel that if you are an award winner your business must be good (which is a reasonable assumption).

Filling in applications and sending in entries can really be time-consuming, hence most businesses don't bother. However, once you have prepared one entry you will probably be able to make minor modifications and use the same submission for other awards.

The publicity and credibility are worth thousands of dollars in free advertising. Be patient—you may not win a prize the first time you enter but eventually you will.

If a potential customer is comparing two businesses and one is a prize winner and one is not, the advantage is definitely with the winner.

If you do win make sure that you tell everyone. Put the certificates on the wall in a prominent place. Include them in the promotional material you send out to potential customers and always include the term 'Award Winning' in your advertisements.

Take the time to enter awards for excellence. Your staff will stand a little straighter and everyone will feel proud. This will rub off on your customers because everyone loves a winner.

18 Call the local radio station

If you have a good relationship with the local radio station and you are proactive in the community you can generally receive some free exposure for your products and services. As discussed in the press release section earlier, free publicity normally only involves a little effort.

Talkback radio is a great way to spread your message by word of mouth. I often contact the local radio station when there is something of significance to discuss. One of our clients is a major shopping centre. If the local radio announcer wants some information about shopping he calls our office and we have a brief conversation on air. Our client gets a free plug and the radio announcer gets the information required in an interesting manner.

Another opportunity exists for businesses to offer to do a free weekly segment on radio. For example, as a marketing consultant, I can approach the local radio station to do a brief session where business operators can ring in and discuss their problems. Hopefully I can offer a few suggestions that will help. My business gets the exposure and the radio station attracts the interest of a market segment they may not already have.

This principle occurs readily on many stations around the world. Some businesses that could really benefit from this type of relationship include:

- accountants offering financial advice;
- medical professionals discussing various ailments;
- lifestyle-based businesses can discuss dealing with modern-day life;
- travel companies can offer to review destinations;
- bookshops can do on-air book reviews;
- mechanical businesses can offer advice on maintaining your car.

19 Ask your customers to tell their friends about you

Satisfied customers are the best form of promotion any business can ever have. How often do you ask your customers the following question: 'Are you happy with the products and the services that we provide?'

If the customer answers 'Yes', then feel free to ask them to tell their family and friends about your business. Most people are very loyal and they are happy to spread the word about a good business but sometimes they need to have someone reminding them to do so.

A number of businesses I have encountered use a sign to pass on this message. Others put it on the back of business cards or cash register receipts, some on invoices and some have their staff ask the question directly.

Earlier in the book (Section 3) I discussed referrals, which are a much more direct way of generating business. By simply asking your customers to recommend your business you are encouraging word-of-mouth advertising without actually asking them to refer a specific friend. This is more applicable to businesses that require a large number of customers coming through the door.

However you choose to ask the question remember to make it light and easy, non-committal and friendly. You can never ask this question too often.

If the customer says they are not happy then you have the potential to find out why and do something about it before you lose them forever. Treat all unhappy customers seriously and settle any disputes quickly and professionally with a minimum amount of fuss.

5 | Are you willing to try a few unusual ideas?

Some of the most successful marketing ideas are somewhat unconventional or unusual. The more traditional forms of media, such as newspapers, radio and television, are often the first to come to mind when people start to plan their advertising but there are many more options that will produce great results, often for a much smaller outlay.

#20   Get behind a wacky promotion
#21   Life in the chicken suit
#22   Enjoy the benefits of 'brainstorming'
#23   Use inflatable toys to build your business
#24   Remember the good old bumper sticker
#25   Use a spruiker to draw in the crowds
#26   Offer prizes in competitions
#27   Get your business in the *Guinness Book of Records*
#28   Use the local pizza company to generate business
#29   Take ownership of an event
#30   Think differently about marketing your business
#31   Use industry publications to collect ideas
#32   Start a marketing ideas box
#33   Take your message on the road with a mobile billboard
#34   Use a blackboard to get attention

20 Get behind a wacky promotion

One of the greatest ideas I have heard about recently was a farmer in England who sold advertising on his cows. A local ice-cream company approached the farmer. They made up blanket-like banners for the cows to wear featuring the message: 'Our main ingredient comes from here' (or something similar to this). The farm was located next to one of England's busiest highways, which meant that tens of thousands of people saw these 'cows with signs' every day.

That was the small part. The advertising cows were so unusual they were featured on television around the world. The ice-cream company received incredible exposure and the cost of the promotion was minimal when you consider the interest it generated.

This is a very clever idea with lots of applications to anyone in business. Every once in a while you may be approached to get involved in some bizarre promotion, such as a kissing competition. We often write these ideas off as being too far from planet earth—well guess again.

Crazy sporting events like *Extreme Games* are viewed by 250 million people around the world. People love crazy— the top rating television shows include *Funniest Home Videos*, *Cops*, *The World's Craziest People* and *Ripley's Believe It Or Not*.

Most of the time when people approach you about getting involved in promotions like this they are after donations of products or time. Don't write these ideas off. Get behind them and make sure that your company name is all over the promotion.

Why don't you be the one to come up with the idea? Make sure it is obtainable and try to get a few people involved in the planning stages to make sure you keep your feet on the ground. The worst that can happen is that you have a lot of fun.

21 Life in the chicken suit

It's corny and somewhat embarrassing but it does work. Walt Disney built an empire on a similar idea. For some reason a person in a crazy suit makes us all smile. If you have no shame (remember no one can recognise you in a clown costume) put on the suit, grab some flyers and hit the streets.

It is a good idea to make the costume relevant to your business and try to make it a good quality suit. A rough homemade job can have the opposite effect and tell people that your business is also a bit rough around the edges. Most cities have someone who makes costumes like this. Once again have a look at previous costumes they have made to make certain that you will receive a professional looking end result.

You can build an entire advertising campaign around the character that you develop. Don't try to be too clever, as the character needs to be instantly recognisable and it should tie in with your business. The aim is to try and get people to think of your business the minute they see the costume figure. Many small businesses have developed a character like this which has gone on to become a prominent feature in parades, at local charity days and during sporting events.

Imagine the free publicity these companies receive. McDonald's is probably the most famous with Ronald McDonald and the team.

When making a costume, once again take the advice of those that are super successful. Don't make the costume too big or kids will be scared. Try to make it easy to get into and out of and as cool as possible. Dress costumes like this can be extremely hot, requiring the people inside to have regular, frequent breaks.

22 Enjoy the benefits of 'brainstorming'

If you want an influx of ideas about what you need to do to increase your business have a brainstorming session. A friend of mine rang me recently inviting me to lunch. She mentioned that there were a few people coming along and she was hoping to generate a few ideas regarding a Lifestyle Expo she was in the midst of planning. As it was a free lunch, how could I say no?

I turned up to a tasteful and quiet restaurant. There were ten people there; most of them I knew but some I did not. There were salespeople, managers, consultants and a few other mixed professions. My friend began the lunch explaining why she had invited everyone there, explaining some of the problems she was experiencing and asking for ideas that would help her Expo to be a success.

The lunch lasted for two hours. My friend left with a list of 44 excellent ideas that would help make the Expo a success. Lunch cost about $300 so for a few hundred dollars and two hours of her time she had a business plan full of fresh ideas donated by professional, intelligent business people.

Perhaps you could do the same thing. A slight variation to this theme is to get ten people together every month and take it in turns brainstorming one business per month. Your turn will come up and, in exchange for giving your time and energy to helping other people solve their business problems, you may solve yours. Every brainstorming session will provide great ideas that can generally be applied to any business, so even if it isn't your turn you may well pick up a few ideas that will help.

By the way, the Expo was held and it was a success.

23 Use inflatable toys to build your business

This form of marketing is growing in popularity, especially over the past two to three years as competition for outdoor signage increases. There is no doubt that having an enormous blow up dinosaur or clown or balloon on your roof will attract attention. These novelties can be hired, once again relatively inexpensively, in most capital cities. They can be used for a grand opening, during a sale or for any other celebration where you want to catch people's attention. They can be particularly effective if your business is located on a major road.

When you realise how much money can be spent on advertising a sale, the novelty idea like the blimp can be a very cost-effective addition to your marketing campaign.

Flags are also popular as they encourage a festive feel to any event and can be seen from quite a distance away.

Blow-up castles are another excellent idea to help build the atmosphere and they also keep the kids occupied while Mum and Dad go shopping.

Unfortunately some balloons and inflatable characters have been used a lot and they start to look very worn, dirty and shabby. Before committing, try to see the inflatable device set up to make certain that all is OK. Another point to check on is local government regulations. Make sure you are allowed to have an inflatable toy on display.

The best place to find these types of novelty items is in the Yellow Pages under 'Promotions', or if you are out and you see an inflatable product that you like, the number will probably be printed on it somewhere. If worst comes to worst, I would recommend walking into the shop being promoted and ask them where they hired the inflatable from.

24 Remember the good old bumper sticker

One of the simplest marketing concepts is the reliable old bumper sticker. While this form of communication is slowly dying as people tend to drive new, sleek-looking cars, there is still life left in the bumper sticker. This is a very cheap and visible way to advertise your business simply by producing a few stickers and handing them out to friends, family and customers.

When making a bumper sticker it can be a good idea to make it funny, nice and colourful and, most important of all, easy to read. Try to keep the words to a minimum and if possible only really use your company name. Another idea is to keep it clean (if you can) as you want to promote a professional image, not a smutty one.

I know a few businesses that offer their customers a discount on products and services in return for a bumper sticker on their car. I have seen a panel beater, an electrician, a tyre seller and a restaurant use this method and they have ended up with hundreds of mini-advertisements driving throughout the city.

Kids love stickers and this is also a way to encourage parents to use your business. They may not be used on car bumpers but there is no doubt that they will be used.

25 Use a spruiker to draw in the crowds

If your business is in the right location, ideally one with plenty of passing traffic, a 'spruiker' can really draw a crowd. Spruikers are the people on the end of the microphone normally used to promote a sale within a store. Sometimes the spruiker will roam from one 'red light special' to another, driving the crowd into a buying frenzy.

Spruikers can be dressed in costume, amplified, animated on video screens or a combination of all, so long as they are good on a microphone and not afraid to interact with the public.

Before employing the services of a spruiker it is always a good idea to check local regulations, particularly if your business is in a shopping centre. There may be limitations on the amount of noise you can make.

One business I know of uses a spruiker to walk around the shopping centre handing out flyers. For an exercise they stopped the spruiker for one month and found that business dropped by 30 per cent. Obviously for this particular company it works and it is considered an essential component of the company's marketing activity.

If you have never used a spruiker before and you are planning a big sale or promotion of some sort, give it some consideration. If you do use a spruiker try and compare figures to a similar sale held previously to determine if it works for your business.

A word of warning: some spruikers are shocking. Try to check them out first. If you get one back to your business and you have the unfortunate experience of finding they are scaring people or using the microphone to chat up passers-by, gently give them the rest of the day off.

26 Offer prizes in competitions

Charities and sporting clubs are always looking for businesses to donate prizes in the form of a sponsorship. Companies that donate goods or services are generally offered exposure in the form of publicity such as logos on promotional material.

When these requests arrive on the fax or over the phone most of us tend to classify them as a minor irritation rather than a marketing opportunity. It is time to retrain those thoughts.

Generally the person seeking sponsorship is after a service or product that your company sells. By donating this you are giving away something with a retail value that you only pay the cost price for. As long as the organisation can offer you good exposure (in writing) this is a good deal. As always, the more publicity the competition or event is promising, the better value you receive for your advertising dollar.

Quite often prizes that you donate are also tax deductible as an advertising expense.

The next time someone calls you asking for a prize or sponsorship, ask yourself the following questions:

- What is the real cost of the prize that you will be donating?
- What publicity will you receive for participating?
- How many people will see your company name (approximately)?
- Can you reach this many people for the cost of the prize with conventional advertising?

Most of the time you will see that these types of sponsorships reach a lot of people, they make your business appear a part of the local community (which it should be) and they return good exposure for a very small outlay.

People love to win things. Most of us rarely win but when we do it's a lot of fun. We live with the hope of winning, hence we buy lottery tickets, gamble at casinos, punt at the races and generally live in hope of winning the big one.

Try sitting down and putting a competition together to encourage people to use your business. There are a few guidelines to consider before embarking on this project:

- Check on gaming regulations to make sure that you can run a competition in your area.
- Make the prize something that you would want to win.
- Make it easy for people to enter.
- Let people enter as many times as they want to.
- Make certain that you promote the competition.

Competitions don't necessarily have to offer huge prizes but they do need to be prizes that people would like to win. A friend of mine owns a country hotel. Every week she gives away a carton of beer and a meat tray in a raffle that is free to enter. This promotion costs her about $50 per week. One of the conditions of winning is that you have to be at the hotel when the prize is drawn somewhere between 5 p.m. and 7 p.m. on the Friday. As you can imagine the pub is crowded and the draw is a big part of the evening.

There is nothing to stop you giving away a prize every week and in some ways lots of small prizes can be better than one big one as you will end up with more happy winners. Quite often sponsors can be found who supply the prizes free of charge in return for the publicity.

Another added bonus of having a competition where people leave their name, telephone number and mailing address is that you now have a mailing list that can be used in direct marketing campaigns.

I have never been to a doctor's surgery where they offer a free consultation as a prize or a mechanic where one lucky customer per week wins a car detailing or a free service and tune-up.

Be imaginative and remember that every person who enters the competition is a potential customer.

27 Get your business in the *Guinness Book of Records*

For those not familiar with the *Guinness Book of Records* it is basically the official record for all manner of facts and figures and outlandish feats. If you want to know anything about the biggest, largest, longest, fastest, heaviest or oldest of anything you will find what you are looking for in the *Guinness Book of Records*.

The publishers of this incredibly popular book travel the world to verify records and record attempts. While they cover all manner of natural phenomenon they also cover all forms of human craziness. If you can get a record into the *Guinness Book of Records* you are virtually guaranteed to get international press coverage.

A client of mine runs a pie making company. This company has been established for a long time and they are trying to sell their pies further afield. For a local promotion they held a free pie day where everyone who came to their bakery received a pie for free and in return they were asked for a gold coin for charity. They raised over $10 000 in one day, which I thought was a fantastic effort. They also received excellent exposure locally.

To get more national awareness they needed an idea that would be different. Hence I suggested making the world's largest meat pie. After our initial research we discovered that to be a world record this pie would have to be over 6 metres in diameter (that's a lot of pie). The size was not the real problem, but finding an oven large enough to fit the pie in was. At the time of writing this book the world's largest pie was still on the drawing board but I have no doubt that it will become a reality that will be seen on television very soon. The pie company is planning to cut the world record pie up and sell pieces for charity. Once again everyone wins.

There really are no limits to what you can do for a

world record. The key is to use your imagination. I recently read about the world's largest guacamole dip. There were a few tonnes of avocados involved and a truckload of corn chips.

One of the great things about making world record attempts is that suppliers are normally happy to get behind these kinds of promotions in return for some recognition.

But don't feel you have to be limited to making something. World records are equally applicable to doing lots of things for long periods of time, such as dancing competitions. The best way to get a feel for the kind of records that you can attempt is to buy a copy of the *Guinness Book of Records* and start working your way through it. With a little bit of planning and good team effort you could be on the front of hundreds of newspapers around the world.

So how do you get in touch with the *Guinness Book of Records*? The best way is via their website at www.guinnessrecords.com

28 Use the local pizza company to generate business

An idea that I came across recently was a convenience store placing promotional flyers in pizza boxes being home delivered. The convenience store promoted their free home delivery service and the fact that they would also deliver a range of items including milk, pet food and alcohol. The convenience store paid the pizza shop per brochure delivered which helped to offset their costs. This idea is quite clever as you are already targeting a customer that is obviously comfortable with the idea of home delivery.

An extension of this idea is to actually print an advertisement on the pizza box. This helps offset the cost of producing the boxes for the pizza restaurant and it ensures that your message is passed on to prospective customers in your geographical region once again.

Talk to your local takeaway service and see what they say. These days many restaurants offer a home delivery service that you might be able to capitalise on. Perhaps this would be another opportunity for a joint venture promotion where you give out their flyers and they give out yours.

29 Take ownership of an event

An event is another name for the celebration of a special occasion of some sort. It can be anything including a wedding, a band in the park, a parade, a concert, a fair, a festival or any one of a thousand other special occasions.

Everyone thinks that to sponsor an event you need to be a major telecommunications company or an airline. This is not true. Once again, look at what big business does. Why do they sponsor events and competitions? Because they receive excellent exposure. The amount of publicity is relative to the value of the sponsorship.

Sponsoring an event can be anything from the local school fete through to the Olympic Games. If it is good enough for the Fortune 500 companies to sponsor events, why shouldn't you?

The degree of sponsorship you contribute to an event could be anything from a few dollars to thousands of dollars. You may be offering sponsorship in the form of goods or services your business produces.

Look at the region you are trying to attract customers from and then look at what events are held periodically and, most importantly, advertised periodically. Send a letter to all of the local schools expressing your interest in sponsoring an event. In return you can offer cash, services or products to a level that will make you the major sponsor. In many instances this may only be a few hundred dollars. Be a bit cheeky and ask for naming rights so that the local beauty pageant now becomes your business name's beauty pageant. For example, the local beauty pageant now becomes 'Jan's Salon Beauty Pageant'.

The exposure you can get from sponsoring events such as this is widespread. Not only are you a good business for supporting a local event but you also get mentioned in advertising for the event, signage at the event, in media

releases for the event and on promotional material produced for the event.

So next time someone comes to talk to you about an
event, have an open mind and look at all of the far-reaching
benefits to your business compared to the minimal outlay
required.

30 Think differently about marketing your business

One of the best pieces of advice I have ever been given (and passed on) is to look outside your own industry for marketing ideas. This may not sound like much of a marketing idea but believe me it is. If you spend all day focusing on what you do and what your competitors do and what your customers do, you can become very insular.

The end result of this is that all businesses within a particular industry start to look the same. For example, have a look at a few dental surgeries. They are all exactly the same. Car rental offices all look the same. Lawyers' offices, doctors, chemists, butchers, bakers and candlestick makers all start to look the same. Is there anything wrong with this? Not really. However, if you look outside of your particular industry you may discover a world of marketing ideas that would work wonderfully for your business.

I experienced this first hand when I had a SCUBA diving shop many years ago. At the time there was a trend for dive shops to be absolutely full of gear, with a fish tank, an old fishing net on the wall with the mandatory plastic fish and crabs and a few pretty cool-looking dudes running the place with earrings and ponytails. My business was struggling. I was very young with absolutely no idea of how to run my own life let alone a business.

To cut a long story short I was desperate. One day a man pulled up in front of the store in a red Porsche. He came inside and introduced himself saying that a friend of mine recommended that he pay me a call. He offered to turn my business around for a flat fee of $5000 (at the time I would have been lucky to have five dollars). I politely said thanks but no thanks.

The months rolled by and business was going from bad to worse. In a bizarre turn of events I joined a lotto syndicate that was advertised in the paper and I won $5000. Rather than paying a few bills I called the guy who had paid me a visit and said that I wanted his help as fast as possible. Of course after I paid him (cash up front I might add) I started to have deep reservations.

My new found saviour came to the shop and spent a few days hanging around and writing things down furiously. He didn't say a word, he just observed. A week later he handed me a small document with a few pages of suggestions for what I should do to turn my business around. As I read through his recommendations my heart sank. His ideas and recommendations were crazy and I thought I was gone.

A few months later I was really on the verge of closing down. I pulled out the document that I had been given earlier and read through the recommendations. The main ones are listed below:

- halve the amount of stock that we carry;
- double the price of everything;
- paint the shop sky blue and hang artwork from the walls;
- introduce a 100 per cent money back guarantee on everything;
- get rid of the ponytails and earrings and put all staff in a suit and tie;
- start selling dive gear on finance;
- offer the absolute best service for everything we do; and
- offer SCUBA tank refills free of charge.

By this stage I had nothing left to lose so I did everything on his list. Basically I turned the store from a dive shop into a 'dive boutique'. Our turnover tripled in the first month. The change was remarkable and I learned probably the most valuable lesson in my business life—the ability to look from the outside in at your business instead of from the inside out (like a goldfish).

Unfortunately I had partnership problems a few months later and the business ended up closing anyway but I knew that it had been turned around. If only I had made the changes six months earlier (or perhaps not had partners).

Why did my business advisor's strange recommendations work? Because he looked at the dive shop as a business, not as a dive shop. The suggestions he made were to fix up an ailing retail business, not an ailing dive shop. In short, he used his experience from all other industries to offer remedies to fix mine.

As a marketing consultant I always find it very easy to offer advice for ailing businesses because their problems are so clear to me. For the people that own these businesses, their days are spent balancing staff, customers, bank accounts, the kids and everything else. It is very difficult to be able to look objectively at what you are doing when you are in the middle of this madness. Hence it is sometimes easier to look at other businesses outside your own industry to see what they are doing and, most importantly, what they are doing well. Look for ideas that you can use and then adapt them to suit your business regardless of whether it is the industry norm. These ideas are not restricted to marketing ideas and they cover anything from the way you answer the phone to the way you serve customers.

By the way, I never saw Mr Red Porsche again and I never had the opportunity to thank him. If by some chance he is reading this I hope it brings a smile to his face.

31 Use industry publications to collect ideas

I subscribe to lots of magazines. It is often hard to find the time to read them all but when I do (normally once per month) I always find practical, helpful business ideas that I can use in my business.

One of the best magazines I receive every month is a specialist marketing magazine. It constantly provides me with a source of ideas to try with my customers and it keeps me informed about the industry as a whole.

Industry publications can contain the answers to many problems that you face on a day-to-day basis. For the minimal cost of a yearly subscription you can be updated on relevant information including access to surveys conducted by the publication and the industry. These surveys can often help you plan your marketing, giving answers to questions like:

- What age group buys my products?
- What is the most successful advertising medium for my product?
- What products are emerging as market leaders?

Other information that will prove invaluable includes consumer trends, new products and technology, information on overseas markets, general business advice, marketing tips, possible suppliers of new products etc.

There are few industries that do not have their own publications to specifically target areas of interest. Often it is simply a matter of tracking down the publication. Information is a powerful business and marketing tool. If you have better information than your competitors then you have the advantage. Subscribe today.

32 Start a marketing ideas box

I often find myself tearing advertisements out of news-papers and magazines, collecting junk mail that has caught my eye or rummaging through boxes of brochures that I have collected over the years. A while back I started to get sick of having all of this hoarded junk falling out of cupboards onto my head so I decided to throw it all away.

As I started to throw the offending material into the bin I discovered that I had a wealth of information including sample advertisements, brochures and marketing ideas that I thought were very, very well done. I culled the pile considerably and ended up with a box of material that has formed the basis of my marketing ideas box (and this book).

Whenever I am stuck for an idea I rummage through the box and invariably I will find an advertisement or a brochure that will suit my intended task perfectly. As I read the papers and magazines that work their way onto my desk I keep a pair of scissors handy to snip out a particu-larly effective or unusual advertisement or an article that may be of use later.

I hate to say this but if the house was on fire this box is the first thing that I would throw to the rescuing fire-fighters (much to my wife's anger). This box stores all the information and ideas that don't fit into my brain.

My advice to you is simple. Start a marketing ideas box today. Continually add to it and continually throw out the junk. If you find yourself buying something based on an advertisement or direct mail letter you received keep it, because if it worked on you, perhaps it can also work for you.

33 Take your message on the road with a mobile billboard

Local government restrictions can limit the size and location of signs in public places. Always consider this before putting any signs in high profile locations. Several years ago I built a mobile billboard. It was exactly the same size as a normal roadside billboard except that I could hook it up to the back of a four wheel drive and tow it all over the city. It was a very high profile advertising tool that I hired out for a daily rate of about $300. The billboard cost approximately $6000 to build so it soon paid for itself.

Now there are a number of companies offering this service. Mobile billboards are an accepted part of any outdoor advertising campaign.

You can always do this on a smaller scale by putting some signs on the side of your average box trailer and parking it near your business. As mentioned, local governments may not be happy about it but in most cases they cannot stop you from doing it. Remember a few points to avoid complaints—don't block driveways or lines of sight on corners, park it out of the way after hours and if someone complains always move the sign.

I adopted these principles when hiring out my mobile billboard and I never had a single complaint. After I sold the business the new operator made a few mistakes. First, the new owner would leave the billboard unattended for days on end, often in public places, blocking lines of sight at intersections and traffic lights. The complaints started to roll in. The next mistake they made was during a promotion for a shopping centre. One centre was advertised on the billboard and the operators of the mobile sign then proceeded to park it in front of a competing centre. This resulted in a lot of complaints, as one would expect, and now the local government authorities will probably ban the mobile billboard operator.

The moral to the story is: if you are doing high profile advertising like a mobile billboard be courteous and considerate, otherwise it will be short-lived. On the upside, mobile billboards are high impact, very visual and relatively inexpensive.

34 Use a blackboard to get attention

Not long ago I was driving to a friend's house for a barbecue. On the way I noticed a huge blackboard on the side of the road outside a local nursery. On the blackboard a message was written: 'Wanted—One wife. Please apply inside.' I thought that this was hilarious and obviously a joke of some sort.

A few days later I picked up the paper and the sign and the man who wrote it were on the front page. That night he was on the news. He really was looking for a wife and he decided to make his intentions rather public. His nursery received so much free publicity that I was almost embarrassed. In the end he found a wife and everyone was happy. All of this happened because of his blackboard on the side of the road. Every time I drive past his business I have to chuckle.

Blackboards instil a sense of spontaneity and value. They are generally used to indicate a special or some other item of interest that changes regularly—hence the need for the blackboard. Restaurants use the blackboard very effectively with most of us being aware of the specials board that tends to be carted from one side of the restaurant to the other throughout the day.

You can use blackboards to the same effect in any business. Put one inside your shop to indicate a daily special. Put a blackboard on the wall outside your business to highlight a new product or a special service. Perhaps make a small sandwich board into a blackboard and put it out the front of your business to draw attention to yourself. Boating companies often put the day's forecast on a blackboard along with a small subliminal message such as sunscreen and refreshments can be purchased on board.

Blackboards are an inexpensive way to get your message across. Remember though that nothing looks worse than a blackboard that looks like it has been written on by a five-year-old child. There are hundreds of people who are chalk artists. They can make up a very professional looking board that you can use or perhaps they can do some graphics and leave the space in the middle for you to update your price or special offer. These chalk artists are inexpensive and if you see a blackboard that has been done professionally and you like the look of it you will probably find the name of the artist in one of the corners.

If you are planning to put a blackboard outside your premises you should check on your local government regulations. Sometimes you will need to have the sign registered.

6 | Do you encourage your staff to build your business?

Good staff are the backbone of any successful business. Unfortunately, most of the time all I ever hear are people complaining about problems with their staff, not their good points. From my experience staff are as good as the training and encouragement they receive. Of course we all make mistakes and hire the wrong people occasionally. The point is that if they are the wrong person, either work on making them the right person or bite the bullet and find the right person.

This section will offer suggestions for increasing the performance of your staff. After all, the better your staff perform the more money your business can make. We'll look at these ideas:

#35   'Can I help you?'—'No thanks, I'm just looking'
#36   Can your staff sell (I mean really sell, not just take orders)?
#37   Ask your staff and your customers to give you their opinions
#38   Offer incentives based on results

35 'Can I help you?'—'No thanks, I'm just looking'

One of the biggest mistakes in business, particularly in retail stores, is the opening conversation. A customer walks in the door, the sales assistant comes over and utters the fatal words, 'Can I help you?'

We all know the immediate response from the customer: 'No thanks, I'm just looking.' This really spells the end of the conversation and the customer has sent a clear message—don't try and sell me something. Now there is tension as the sales assistant hovers close by waiting to assist, the customer feels like they are going to be pounced on and in a short amount of time they leave.

We have all experienced this interaction either from the customer's point of view or the sales assistant's point of view or perhaps both. Anyone who has ever travelled to Bali will fully appreciate what it feels like to be under pressure to buy. I loathe it.

I walked into a clothing store recently. It was very large, with at least seven or eight sales staff milling around. A young man started walking towards me and I immediately prepared myself for the 'No thanks, I'm just looking' response. The sales assistant walked up to me and said, 'Good morning, sir. Is this your first visit to our store?' I was somewhat stumped by this question and I answered honestly that, yes, it was my first visit. The young man then explained the layout of the shop, where men's clothing was, formal and casual, and then he showed me the specials racks and quietly said that there were some real bargains to be found here. Before I could say anything else he asked me if he could excuse himself as he had to prepare an order but if I wanted some help just wave and he would be straight over. Then he asked me if I had any questions. I quietly said no and began to shop—feeling completely at home and relaxed.

As I shopped I noticed the same interaction happening with each customer that walked in. All of the sales assistants took the same approach and the result was amazing. If someone appeared to be a regular shopper in the store the sales assistant gave them a brief update on specials, new items or lines and then left the customer to his or her own devices.

The manager of this shop is, in my opinion, a very smart person. The sales staff were excellent and the customers were free to shop without an ounce of pressure. The majority of people don't like being pounced on when they first walk into a shop. They want a bit of time to get the feel of the place, perhaps have a quick look around and then ask for assistance.

Another way to help make contact with the customer without putting them under pressure is to give them something. A friend of mine owns a large gallery. I have watched people enter the gallery and shy away as the staff members lunge at them. In this case I suggested he make a small map of the gallery that staff members can give to people when they enter. It is an easy icebreaker and it provides the opportunity for a light conversation with no pressure on the customers.

Retailing is a complicated and involved form of business. Too many people think that it is simply a matter of opening up a shop and waiting for the customers to flock in. I have rarely seen it work this easily. Every detail is important—from the colour of the walls to the type of products you will sell to the prices you plan to charge. Very few shops get it right straight away with most having to spend months if not years fine tuning the details to get everything right. The upside is that when they do get it right these businesses can be very profitable.

Another interesting point to note is that the position of the counter can have a huge bearing on the sales within a shop. A client of mine owns a well-known national handbag and fashion accessories shop. The counter in the shop was initially right in front of the door so people had to walk straight to the counter if they wanted to go into the shop. Realising that this was a problem he moved the counter to the back of the shop and business increased by over 35 per cent.

Try a new approach to dealing with customers as they walk in and see the results. Some experts suggest that many retail businesses could increase their revenue by up to 30 per cent simply by never asking the infamous 'Can I help you?' question. Try it today.

36 Can your staff sell (I mean really sell, not just take orders)?

One of the greatest tragedies that I witness in most businesses I visit is that the people serving don't know how to sell. Very few businesses have well trained sales staff.

There is no way that this book can possibly address the detailed area of sales—thousands of other books around the world do—but there is one issue that I can address. If you spend thousands of dollars setting up your business, purchasing stock, advertising and marketing your heart out only to have a potential customer walk through the door and then walk out the door because the sales attendant couldn't close the sale, why bother?

Sales attendants should be able to recommend a product to any customer based on their individual needs. They should also be able to up sell. If a customer buys a fishing reel, how about some new fishing line and, while you're at it, how about some hooks, sinkers, bait, a new rod, Esky, hat, book and a boat to put it all in.

If someone has walked through the door there is a good chance they want to make a purchase. It is up to whoever is serving that customer to help them make the purchase and leave your business feeling satisfied and happy, to the point where they will not only return but also recommend you to their friends.

Spend a few dollars and enrol your staff in a sales training course. Talk to other people in business to find a recommended course or trainer they may have used. Give your front-line staff the skills and expertise to sell your products to the best of their advantage. Saving a few dollars by using inexperienced and untrained staff is not only false economy but a sure-fire way to go broke.

McDonald's annual sales are increased by a staggering $200 million per year simply because the staff are trained to ask customers if they would like a drink and some fries with their order.

In my opinion there are ten key attributes that make a good salesperson. These are:

1. they smile and have a sense of humour;
2. they are naturally friendly;
3. they are always polite;
4. they always follow-up;
5. they are always well dressed;
6. they ask their customers what they want;
7. they look for ways to save their customers money;
8. they offer an opinion or a recommendation;
9. if they can't help they tell the customer who can; and
10. they ask for the sale.

If your staff are not good salespeople don't blame them until you have given them the necessary tools to be able to sell. How much could you increase your bottom line if your staff were trained to make that extra sale?

Put as much time and effort into grooming your staff as you do into grooming your shop and you will be amazed at the results.

37 Ask your staff and your customers to give you their opinions

We all get too close to our own businesses. A fresh pair of eyes can often identify creative and innovative ways to market and promote your business.

Putting a suggestion box in your workplace is another one of those ideas that people sometimes cringe at. But take heart, there are people with some fantastic ideas on how to improve your business and some of them may be working for you or some may already be your customers.

Putting in a suggestion box takes away any pressure that a person may feel when voicing their opinion. Fear of rejection or ridicule often prevents staff members from suggesting ideas. It is a confidential way to have your say.

I have a number of clients who run very open businesses. They constantly ask their staff, customers, friends and even their bank managers for opinions on all aspects of their business but particularly marketing. I think that they are very clever operators because in the end they get the benefits of any good ideas that are suggested.

I was recently talking to clients who run a restaurant. They wanted to cater more for families and we were discussing the introduction of a children's menu that could be coloured in. At the same time we were discussing making cardboard hats to give to children when they leave the restaurant. A member of the team suggested combining all three ideas into a hat with the children's menu and a colouring-in section on one side and a bright cartoon printed on the other. Another great idea was born. We produced the hats and they are a great hit.

Asking staff and customers for their opinion is also an excellent way to get an honest appraisal on how your business is performing. You can use a suggestion box or you can write to people and ask for their opinion or sometimes it is appropriate to give them a call and ask, 'What do you think of this?'

An important point to remember is that you asked for their opinion and that is exactly what they are giving you. Sometimes you might not like what they have to say but maybe you need to hear it. I always appreciate someone telling me about a weakness in my business. I prefer it when they compliment me on a strength but that's life.

I would love to give my opinion about any business that I feel is offering either a fantastic service or a lousy one.

38 Offer incentives based on results

Many business operators believe that paying a person a wage should be incentive enough for them to perform at their peak. Unfortunately this is generally not the case. Most businesses could increase revenue dramatically if their staff sold more product. Once your staff know how to sell try giving them an incentive to sell—your business will ultimately receive the benefits.

Incentives can take three forms:

1. financial;
2. recognition; and
3. responsibility.

1. Financial Offer your staff some form of financial benefits to sell more. I have worked in several companies where some staff have been on salary only and some are on a salary plus commission. Without exception far better sales were achieved from the people on a salary plus commission.

The reality of the situation is that people are generally far more concerned with their own financial wellbeing than the financial wellbeing of the company they are working for—it's human nature. If you can structure a financial incentive for your staff based on their performance you may be surprised by the increase in sales.

2. Recognition Implement a staff member of the month scheme. If your business does not have a recognition program like this think about instigating one. Research often shows that people want to feel important. You can do this by saying thank you for a job well done. If you can offer a prize of some sort all the better. Once again look at the large companies like McDonald's. Whenever you walk in the door there is a photo of the staff member of the month, in a high profile position. Imagine how proud that individual staff member will feel.

I have seen companies offer great rewards for outstanding staff members. A very large hotel that I know offers the best car park in the building to the staff member of the month. It is theirs to use for the month of their award. Another offers the staff member of the month their choice of shifts for the entire month. Some companies offer pamper packages including massages, haircuts, manicures etc. for the staff member of the month.

The key to offering successful recognition prizes is to tailor make them for your particular business. Something as small as a couple of movie tickets or a box of chocolates to say thank you can really go a long way.

3. Responsibility Many staff are motivated by increasing their position within the company. Increased responsibility is often a major motivator. Unfortunately, most business people spend half their working day trying to offload their responsibilities to reduce their stress. Because of this they tend to forget that many of their staff may be yearning for some extra responsibility.

I have often seen a mediocre staff member blossom into a key member of staff once they were given the responsibility. If someone is doing a good job and deserves recognition, give them a title. People love titles and the extra sense of responsibility they bring. Instead of a Sales Attendant perhaps upgrade them to a Senior Sales Executive. In recent years the title of 'Director' has become very popular. Larger companies have 'Director of Sales and Marketing', 'Director of Operations' and 'Director of Administration'.

If your staff are happy they will sell more and they will offer better service to your customers. Everybody wins.

7 | Do you make it easy for people to buy from you?

This is an area I feel very passionate about. I can never understand why some businesses seem to make it hard to buy things from them. Recently we were buying a pile of furniture to fit out our new office. We went to one furniture store to try and buy the lot and it was nothing but grief. They had a table that we were interested in but it wasn't assembled for us to look at. If we wanted to see it assembled we would have to pay a $500 deposit (I'm not sure how we could have damaged it by looking at it). What made it worse was that this $500 deposit would not be refunded. Instead we would be given a $500 credit to purchase other items in the shop if we didn't want the table. Yeah, right.

We went straight up the road and purchased thousands of dollars worth of furniture on the spot at a shop where the owner went out of her way to help us. The moral to the story is that if you make it hard for people to buy your products and services they will go somewhere else. I am constantly amazed at how many businesses seem to specialise in being difficult. In this section we'll investigate the following ways to make it easy:

#39   Pick up the cost of the call
#40   The perfect gift for the indecisive customer
#41   Don't make it hard for people to give you money
#42   Make life easy for parents—cater for their kids

39 Pick up the cost of the call

Freecall numbers (where you pay for the incoming call) are not expensive and I suggest that any business wanting to expand into a larger geographical region should arrange for this service immediately. The actual number can be linked to any existing line and you receive a monthly statement detailing how many calls the free phone number received and where they originated.

The cost to establish this service can vary. From my experience the telecommunications companies are a lot more negotiable these days so it is worth asking for a special price or one-off discount.

Once you have your Freecall number don't be afraid of handing it out and giving it to your customers—after all that's what it's for. Have it printed on your brochures, business cards, everywhere. It makes your business look very professional and gives the impression that you care enough about your customers to pay for their phone calls.

I have three Freecall numbers. Two for telephone lines and one for a fax line. One of the Freecall numbers is for a publication we produce. Our advertiser client base is spread out over a large geographical region. The majority of phone calls on this line are from people wanting to advertise. Based on our research many of these people would not have rung if we did not have a Freecall number. The monthly bill for this line is about $200 and we calculate that we receive almost $3000 per month worth of business from the Freecall line. Whichever way you look at it it makes sense.

In even simpler terms, imagine a potential client is looking at two advertisements—one for your business and one for a competitor. Both businesses will require a long distance call at the most expensive time of day. If you have the Freecall number and your competitor does not, I strongly believe that the customer will ring your business.

Freefax numbers work exactly the same way as Freecall numbers. This is an excellent way to encourage your customers to stay in touch and to keep faxing those bookings through. If your business relies heavily on facsimile transmissions for orders then take a few moments to seriously consider getting a Freefax number.

Perhaps you have existing clients that give you a lot of business, all sent through by the facsimile. Imagine how they would feel if you sent them a thank you letter saying how much you appreciate the business. You have calculated that they send through 200 faxes per year at a cost of $1.50 per fax—resulting in a total cost to their business of $300. As a way to show your gratitude, from now on you are providing them with a Freefax number so that their communications costs will be dramatically reduced.

I would be very impressed if someone made that offer to my company. The extra business you can generate by showing initiative in a situation like this will more than offset the extra costs associated with your Freefax or Freecall lines. And if your Freecall bill is high, imagine the orders that have been coming through.

Everyone wants to feel important as a customer. In this rapidly-growing world the difference between success and failure is customer service.

40 The perfect gift for the indecisive customer

Most large companies sell gift vouchers. This makes buying a generic present easy and it enables the end recipient of the gift voucher to purchase exactly the item they want.

There are a number of options when it comes to producing your own gift vouchers. If you are handy with your computer make up your own and print them out on nice paper. You can also buy pre-printed gift vouchers from most larger stationery stores where you simply fill in your business details and the amount of the voucher. Another option, if they prove to be successful, is to design and print your own.

If you decide to offer gift vouchers it is important to let your customers know—put a sign up, send out a flyer to regular customers or put a flyer into any bag or parcel that leaves your store. There is no point offering gift vouchers if your customers don't know about them.

Another extension of this idea is a generic gift voucher that is accepted at more than one business. Shopping centres often do this. You can purchase a gift voucher at any store and the person receiving the voucher can redeem it at any store in the centre. This can be a little complicated to coordinate but it increases the appeal of the voucher as the customer receiving the gift can make their purchases at the store (or stores) of their choice.

One word of caution—gift vouchers are like money so make certain that you do not leave them lying around unsecured. Also put a code of some sort on the vouchers that lets you know they are authentic. Numbered vouchers enable you to track down who made the purchase and who redeemed the vouchers.

41 **Don't make it hard for people to give you money**

In these technical days there really is no reason not to accept all major credit cards and in most cases EFTPOS. Many people choose to pay all of their accounts on a credit card and then pay that amount in full at the end of the month. For many this is an excellent way to accrue frequent flyer points without actually flying and for others it is a way of reducing mortgage payments.

When making large purchases, such as computers, furniture or accommodation and airfares, I always use my American Express card because I earn frequent flyer points. I can also use this card for the majority of my business expenses including telephone, stationery, petrol, printer cartridges and much more. Normally at the end of the year the resulting frequent flyer points are enough for my wife and I to have a holiday.

Keeping this in mind, if faced with the option of using a business that takes American Express and one that does not, assuming that the prices are similar, I will always use the business that accepts the card. I speak to many other business people in a similar situation and they all say the exact same thing. Are you missing out on good business simply because you don't offer enough payment options?

Advertising the fact that you will take payments over the phone is another important point. If you don't mention it people may not ask. If you take personal cheques, advertise that fact as well.

Make it easy for people to do business with you.

42 Make life easy for parents—cater for their kids

The world's leading fast food chains have certainly got this idea well and truly under control. McDonald's restaurants have fast become playgrounds with a restaurant attached. Parents can take their children to a McDonald's and not only is everyone fed but they are also entertained. What a brilliant idea.

Look at ways that your business can become more child-friendly. Putting in a small playground may seem like an expensive idea but at the end of the day the costs can be more than offset by an increase in business.

Catering for kids can be anything from a television to a blow-up castle or toys in a playpen. Like all of the marketing ideas in this book, I suggest that you cater for kids according to your budget.

If you start to look around you will see more and more businesses adopting a 'catering for children' attitude. I have noticed it being used in clubs, restaurants, theatres, shopping centres, department stores, furniture shops and electrical goods retailers.

Why not make up a cheap colouring-in book to give to children visiting your business. Remember the kids' packs that airlines hand out? The same principle could apply to many other businesses. When I worked for a cruise ship company we developed a kids' pack that had a starfish, some fish stickers, a ruler, some colouring-in pencils and a colouring-in book, which was handed to all children as they came on board.

Remember that there are a lot of potential customers who have kids and sometimes they need to take them shopping. Become a market leader and cater for children in your industry before your competition does and you will receive the benefits.

As my editor pointed out, there are now shops, cafes and restaurants that openly display signs in their windows advertising that they are 'breastfeeding friendly' and that nursing mothers are welcome. Any mother with a baby in tow would welcome this sign that once again encourages parents into a business rather than scaring them off.

Many countries have stores that even cater for pets so that if people are taking their dog for a walk and they decide to do some shopping, there is a special pet room with food and water, play toys and even cages for the more antisocial animals. The pet owners can shop at leisure knowing that little 'Lassie' is being well looked after.

8 | Do you have smart, hard-hitting promotional material?

Every business should have good promotional material. Often your brochures and flyers are the first point of contact a potential customer may have with your business. If your promotional material doesn't inspire them to use your business then it is a waste of time. This section will outline some of the ways to make more effective promotional material that will produce greater results for your business. We'll look at:

#43   The bolder the heading the bolder the response
#44   Making your first brochure
#45   Make up an information booklet to give to customers
#46   Always be prepared to hand out a brochure
#47   Build credibility with testimonials from happy customers
#48   Start your own newsletter
#49   Clever promotional material costs no more
#50   How to always be under your customers' noses

43 **The bolder the heading the bolder the response**

The heading is everything when it comes to making brochures, flyers or advertisements for newspapers and magazines. Ninety per cent of the time devoted to preparing an advertisement or a flyer should be spent planning the heading. If you don't catch a person's attention within a few seconds you have wasted your time and money.

The heading needs to big, bold and easy to read and understand. A common mistake with most advertising is that the person making the advertisement tends to put about five hundred words into the space of a business card.

These days consumers are busy. There is enormous competition and advertisements need to catch the potential customer's eye first and foremost and then they will read the information contained within the brochure or advertisement.

The way to catch attention is with the heading. Make it short, sharp and sweet. Whenever you are planning an advertisement or producing a flyer take a few minutes to flick through a national newspaper and look at some advertising done by the giant corporations. Try to overcome the need to put too much text into your promotional material and make the heading really stand out.

To complement big, bold headings you need to leave plenty of space around the heading to make certain that it does stand out. The other old saying is that white space sells. While there are those who firmly believe that advertisements filled with text can work, my experience has shown they fail more often than they succeed.

I suggest starting a scrapbook for advertisements that catch your eye. Cut them out and use their principles next time you make an advertisement or flyer.

44 Making your first brochure

Promotional material is an important component of any marketing strategy—it reflects your business and customers will often decide whether or not they are going to use a particular business simply by looking at the company brochure.

Brochures can vary from a single-page one-colour flyer right through to a full colour, glossy magazine-style brochure. It all depends on your budget and the end use that the brochure is being produced for. Both styles can be very effective. One-page flyers can have a number of uses.

If you are not sure how to go about making a brochure the first step is to decide what type of promotional material you like. Keep your eyes open and whenever you see a brochure that you like, take a copy and file it away. When you find one that you really like, take it to a graphic designer and tell them that you want a brochure similar to this.

The actual process of producing and designing a brochure can be done by desktop publishers and graphic designers. There are a few simple guidelines to follow:

- To find a graphic designer ask other business associates for a recommendation. Ask to see samples of their work.
- Shop around and compare prices.
- Agree on a price before the job commences so that you are 100 per cent aware of all costs involved.
- Make certain you use good quality photographs in any promotional material.
- Use the best paper that you can afford. Thicker paper does not increase printing costs by much but the end result is a higher quality brochure.

The last point is worth discussing. The type of paper that your brochure is printed on is important. This is called the stock. The thicker the stock the better quality your brochure will feel. The cost does not increase much when it comes to increasing stock. Whenever you are getting quotations for printing brochures always get some extra prices for the option of increasing the stock.

The cover of any brochure is the most important part. If it does not inspire potential customers to either pick it up or read it then you have wasted your money. Use pictures where possible and keep the writing to a minimum. Show the draft version of the brochure to a few friends to get their opinion.

It is easy to get too close to a brochure making objectivity very difficult. Showing other people will also highlight any spelling mistakes or other errors that are easy to miss when you have read a passage a hundred times.

One of the most important tips I have learned from producing a lot of printed material is to always sleep on it before sending the final job to print. Look at the artwork when you are fresh and relaxed, not at the end of a frantic day when you are rushing to get the job into an air bag and onto the last plane. A printed mistake will last forever and, really, a day here or there rarely makes that much of an impact on a deadline. Leave yourself plenty of time to make certain that you are not under pressure when it comes to producing your promotional material.

45 Make up an information booklet to give to customers

I was recently approached by a large building company to develop a marketing idea they could use to promote their new services for building maintenance and inspection works. During a meeting that lasted for 30 minutes I was constantly having to stop and ask technical questions regarding terminology of the building trade. I was fascinated by the government regulations regarding maintenance and building inspection work and the cost involved to the property owners.

Then it dawned on me that most people would be blissfully ignorant of the fact that extensive maintenance can save you a fortune, even on the family home. I suggested they produce an information booklet regarding home maintenance in simple, easy-to-read and easy-to-understand language. Once it was written copies could be given to everyone.

This booklet will prove to be very informative to the individual who wants to protect their largest investment. The building company can promote their services throughout the booklet, with the end result being that prospective customers have good literature provided for free by a company that can solve all of their maintenance worries.

Once again this concept can be adapted to virtually any industry. Electricians could make an information booklet about maintenance of home appliances, the local nursery could make a booklet on caring for pot-plants, the local butcher could give you recipes for cooking their products (most already do) and so on.

If a booklet is too daunting, why not make up a one-page flyer answering the ten most frequently asked questions about a particular product or service. Advertise your business name on the bottom of the flyer and hand it to everyone visiting your shop.

Remember to keep it simple, informative and easy to read and don't be embarrassed about flying your company flag throughout the booklet—after all, you paid for it.

46 Always be prepared to hand out a brochure

I always find it hard to understand when I meet someone and they don't have a business card or a company brochure with them. The only excuse for this is if you are on a surfboard somewhere off Maui (but the keen business person would probably have waterproof business cards just for this exact situation).

Some business operators almost seem embarrassed to fly their own flag and tell complete strangers all about the business they are in. Part of owning or operating a business is marketing it and one of the best ways to market it is to talk to people. I have struck up conversations with complete strangers while standing in a queue and before you know it they are telling me they own a large company and they need a marketing company to do some work for them.

I always carry business cards, brochures, copies of my books and anything else that can help me to get more business. Leave a boxful in the boot of the car. Load up your briefcase—you never know who you will meet. Leave some brochures at home just in case someone comes over to dinner and they want some information about your business to give to a friend or colleague.

Always be prepared to take advantage of a situation that could bring you more business. It doesn't mean that you have to start stalking people but it does mean that you should always be prepared for an impromptu opportunity to sell yourself.

How often do you get asked, 'What do you do for a living?' Don't be shy about promoting your business to complete strangers—after all, every customer begins as a complete stranger.

47 Build credibility with testimonials from happy customers

Testimonials are statements from your customers saying how great your business is. They are very good marketing tools and they should be used in your promotional material wherever possible.

Whenever we finish a major project it is standard procedure to ask the client for a testimonial. We ask them to be honest and to tell us the good and the bad points of dealing with us and we welcome any suggestions for improving our services. It is a kind of debriefing. Fortunately most of our testimonials are excellent and we show these to prospective customers who are thinking about using our services. Without a doubt these testimonials help to generate most of our work.

The things you are looking for in a testimonial are comments that emphasise that your company is reputable, professional, reliable and honest. When using testimonials in your printed material always include a name and where the person comes from. Copies of letters sent in by happy customers are even more helpful. It is amazing how many companies have boxes full of letters from customers saying how great they are but they never use them.

Don't make up your own testimonials and if possible you should check with the person supplying the testimonial to see if it is OK to use it in your promotional material. A great way to get testimonials from your customers is with a guest book on the counter.

Testimonials should always be used in advertising and the nicest thing about them is that they are absolutely free; all you have to do is provide good service and ask your customers for a few words.

A sample testimonial follows:

101 Ways To Market Your Business helped to turn my business around. The information contained in it is relevant, up-to-date and very easy to implement. I think your book is great and every small business owner should have a copy.'

Mr John Doe, Upper Reaches, Timbuktu

Use testimonials as often as possible. Put them in your advertisements, on flyers, in brochures, even on the wall of the office.

48 Start your own newsletter

Another great idea is to start your own newsletter. If you have established a good database of past clients, why not take the time to produce a newsletter once a month or once every few months to keep your customers updated on what is happening in your business and in your industry.

I see hundreds of businesses that could really benefit from this type of promotion but they rarely do because it is too hard to think of new ideas and to get someone to write it. Remember, newsletters are exactly that—a brief letter telling the news. They do not need to be works of art or fifty pages long but they do need several elements to be successful:

1. newsletters must be well laid out and easy to read;
2. they need a few pictures or line drawings;
3. they must come out regularly;
4. the information must be relevant and accurate;
5. the writing must be interesting;
6. try to be light and humorous;
7. articles should be short and to the point; and
8. encourage people to contribute articles to the newsletter.

I used to buy my fishing equipment at a store in Western Australia several years ago. This business started a monthly newsletter and I could not wait for it to arrive each month. It contained excellent information that was very relevant. The fishing newsletter had pictures of the best catches that month, a brief product review of new fishing rods and reels, an article on bait by one of the staff, the next month's tide charts, advertisements for fishing charters and a schedule for any fishing television shows being aired during the next month.

What a great newsletter. The icing on the cake was that a fishing equipment manufacturer sponsored the newsletter, paying for all costs in return for an advertisement. The amount of business generated by this simple procedure was immeasurable. Perhaps your business could benefit from a customised newsletter.

Talk to a desktop publisher and agree on a price to produce a newsletter once a month. Print it out on a laser printer on nice paper and start sending it out. Ask your customers if they like it and develop the newsletter based on their feedback. Try and get your suppliers to pay the costs.

If you don't know where to start, try to find a newsletter that you like the look of and see if you can adapt it to your needs. An important tip here is to be careful about overcommitting your time. It is better to do a newsletter every three months religiously than to say you will bring it out monthly and then not be able to because of other commitments or a lack of information.

49 Clever promotional material costs no more

One of the best marketing ideas I have seen was in a motel. The 'Do not disturb' sign was sponsored by the local takeaway pizza restaurant. They obviously provided the motel with the signs free of charge. They were very professional and colourful and the home delivery service number was clearly visible. Perhaps your business could be offering the same type of product at the local motel. This could be anything from a taxi company to a beauty salon.

Contact any motels in your area and talk to them. Even if they do not want signs for the door they may have a compendium of local information where you can put your brochure or flyer at no cost.

The cable television companies have developed a similar idea with a card that fits over the door handle and passes on the message that they called in to discuss connecting the cable but no one was home. Perhaps you could apply a similar marketing idea to your business.

The underlying message here is that clever ideas stand out and produce results. Think about your marketing, try to be different and stay one step ahead of your competitors.

50 How to always be under your customers' noses

A clever idea that is starting to become widely used is to have message pads printed as free giveaways for your customers or potential customers. These message pads contain advertising about your business, detailing your range of products and services and contact details.

A printing company I use gives away telephone message pads. On the notepad the printer has their telephone number and a small list covering the type of products that they produce. Every office uses message pads and the printer cleverly made the pads easy to read, self-carbonating and in books of about one hundred messages. Every time someone in the office takes or gives a message the printing company receives the exposure.

If you decide to make something like this always ensure that it is good quality and practical for people to use. Keep your company message brief and subtle.

A larger version of the message pad is the desk planner. These are the large pads of about 50 sheets that you use to write on. They normally have a calendar on the side and plenty of blank spaces for writing notes. They are quite large, about the size of six normal sheets of paper joined together.

While a desk planner is a more expensive option there is a lot more room to promote your company message. We have made a number of desktop planners for our clients and the response has been excellent.

Any item that will be used often by a customer has to be worth looking at. How many rulers and pens do you get given that promote various company messages? I get given quite a few and if they are good quality I tend to use them.

9 | Would you like to make everyday advertising ideas work for your business?

Conventional marketing ideas are an essential component of any marketing plan. There are of course ways that you can increase your results when using these conventional marketing ideas. This section looks at ways to increase the effectiveness of your everyday advertising. We'll look at:

#51   Work with other businesses and promote each other

#52   Making the most of Yellow Pages advertising

#53   Tickets please

#54   Making a newspaper advertisement that works

#55   Using the cinema to spread the word

#56   Making a cheap television commercial that works

#57   Bus advertising—inside and out

#58   Booking quality television, newspaper and radio advertising space

#59   Use cheap classified advertisements to generate business

#60   Get your suppliers to assist with your advertising

#61   Tap into large membership-based organisations

#62   Making a radio advertisement that works

#63   Free local newspapers can produce plenty of work

#64   Everyone gets one of these at the supermarket

51 Work with other businesses and promote each other

Cooperative advertising has many shapes and forms. Working with other businesses to jointly promote both businesses can be very effective. It provides a way to save money and to make your marketing budget go further.

For example, two retail shops that I frequent have reached an agreement. One is a shoe store and one is a menswear shop. Each business hands out the other's promotional flyers to any customer that makes a purchase. The businesses concerned are not conflicting and they both serve about the same number of customers. The cooperative promotion goes one step further where customers are offered a 10 per cent discount for shopping at the cooperative company's store.

This type of promotion can be effective. There is no reason why you could not have multiple cooperative marketing partners, as long as each business benefits.

Another example of this is at the local shopping centre where everyone who makes a purchase at the chemist receives a voucher for a free cappuccino coffee at a particular restaurant. The restaurant gets the extra business as a result of people coming in to redeem their vouchers and staying for a meal. The chemist gets extra business because everyone wants a free cup of coffee. This is the classic win–win situation where both stores are happy and the customer feels important and special because someone has taken the time to offer them something for free.

Theme parks and tourist attractions offer special passes where one ticket can cover admission to three or more attractions. There is a cost advantage in buying the special pass which gives the consumer incentive to buy the all-inclusive pass, and the companies involved get to spread their marketing budget more widely to attract more customers.

Most businesses could form some kind of cooperative marketing allegiance. I recently noticed an advertisement where a seafood restaurant and a seafood market made a joint television commercial. The seafood restaurant explained how their key to success was the exceptional quality of the seafood that they purchased from the seafood market. Both companies are promoted for half the cost.

Coffee shops always work with coffee suppliers. The supplier provides machines, umbrellas, signage and even cups and the coffee shop buys their coffee. Many restaurants work in similar ways with wine suppliers.

Cooperative advertising has benefits for everyone involved. You can always work with more than one other business and in fact I often encourage three or four businesses that are non-conflicting to work together to promote their services. This makes their marketing budgets go much further and it creates more interest for the customer.

Cooperative advertising is only limited by imagination. Always be on the lookout for novel ways to work with other businesses that will benefit all involved.

52 Making the most of Yellow Pages advertising

Yellow Pages advertising is without doubt very effective. Most businesses need to be featured in the Yellow Pages but many resent having to put an advertisement in this publication.

I know a lot of companies that only advertise in the Yellow Pages—it's their entire marketing budget. If this is the case you need to be certain that it is going to work. Most advertisements in the Yellow Pages are hastily put together, often difficult to read and sometimes confusing.

First, if you are going to go to the effort and expense of putting an advertisement into the Yellow Pages, pay the extra money and get a graphic artist to design the advertisement. Make it easy to read and have a good heading. If possible include a photograph of a person (research shows that advertisements with people have a much higher success rate than those without).

Your telephone number doesn't need to be enormous—it is after all a telephone book so the customer knows that your phone number will be in the advertisement somewhere.

Put a wide border around the advertisement, leave plenty of space around your message and perhaps even include a 100 per cent money back guarantee to further encourage the customer to call you.

Further to this, I always encourage businesses to take the biggest advertisement they can afford. To monitor the success of your advertisement, why not get a phone connected with a number unique to the Yellow Pages advertisement so that you will know exactly how many calls you receive each week.

The continual debate over whether to go for a colour advertisement or not is probably up to you. If you have a good, clean advertisement with plenty of space around the edges you don't need colour. I also believe that the extra cost is better spent on upgrading the size of your advertisement.

Quite often I hear people complaining that an advertisement didn't work. The business blames the publication. Nine times out of ten I look at the advertisement and it is a jumbled mass of information that is hard to read, has too much colour and too many words.

Very few businesses take the time to ask their customers how they heard about their business so they don't really know if their advertisements are working or not.

I often flick through directories like the Yellow Pages and newspapers to see what type of advertisements catch my eye. You can try doing the same thing. If it stands out enough to catch your eye try to determine what made it so effective.

One funny story I heard recently was about an American phone book. A takeaway pizza company was offering a free pizza for anyone who brought in another pizza restaurant's advertisement cut out from the Yellow Pages. The end result is clear—but as you would expect there were a few very unhappy pizza shop owners in the area.

The point I am making is to put a lot of thought into your advertising. Take the time to do a good advertisement, not a rushed, jumbled mess that is guaranteed to have no result. Yellow Pages is relatively expensive but very effective for most businesses.

53 Tickets please

Advertising on the back of admission tickets is a good promotion because everyone involved wins. You pay for the tickets to be produced and perhaps make an offer of some sort to encourage customers to visit your business. The business that gives out the tickets hands them to their clients, increasing your chances of them visiting your business.

The company handing out the tickets doesn't have to pay for the printing of the tickets and your business gets exposure to hundreds or perhaps potentially thousands of customers.

A good idea I saw recently for this was a late-night cafe/restaurant advertising on the back of cinema tickets. To further sweeten the deal the cafe was offering a free cappuccino with every slice of cake purchased. This deal proved too good for me to bypass.

Some of the businesses that use admission tickets include car parks, theme parks, buses, trains, ferries and theatres, to mention just a few. Give them a call and see if they would be interested in saving money by letting you advertise on the back of their admission tickets.

Perhaps your business could benefit from advertising on the back of these admission tickets.

54 Making a newspaper advertisement that works

Newspaper advertisements can be very effective. Unfortunately they can also be expensive, depending on the publication. Like any marketing idea, I suggest you should tailor your newspaper advertising around your budget. The bigger the advertisement, the bigger the results tend to be.

Newspaper advertising is good to promote items that call for immediate action. By this I mean the customer reads the advertisement and they can do something about it today. It might be a sale on at the local shopping centre, a new movie, a new car, a house or a restaurant. Newspapers bring instant results and because of this you need to tailor your advertisement to make the most of this characteristic.

The following list identifies ways to increase your success in newspaper advertisements.

1. always have a strong heading to catch the readers' attention;
2. design unusually sized advertisements;
3. keep words to a minimum;
4. try to leave space in the advertisement;
5. use a border;
6. give the person a reason to call you immediately;
7. only use pictures if they have a lot of contrast—newspaper print is the lowest quality you can get so be careful when using pictures; and
8. make sure you include all the facts—who, what, when, where.

Positioning of your advertisement is also important. Some people swear that your advertisement should be on a right-hand page and preferably an early right-hand page (up the front of the newspaper), which is why you pay more for these spaces. I don't necessarily agree with this; however, it is a matter of trial and error. The more often you place an advertisement the more likely you are to get results. Follow the above guidelines and you will increase your chances of producing a successful newspaper advertisement.

55 Using the cinema to spread the word

The greatest attraction of the cinema from a marketing point of view is the fact that they have a lot of people passing through. The cinema attracts customers with disposable income and many other businesses need to attract these customers as well.

The advertisements we watch before the movie are growing in popularity once gain. The image of cinema advertising has undergone vast improvements in the past few years with new look commercials produced by state-of-the-art graphic designers. One of the best features of cinema advertising is that you can choose which movies you would like to be featured in. This enables you to target a specific audience that a particular movie would attract.

Like most advertising, the costs are negotiable. The key to success is good placement of your advertisements and having a good visual picture. I am a firm believer that to be remembered you really need to be funny or you need to make a sensational offer with this type of advertising.

Businesses that are close to a cinema could benefit the most from cinema advertising. Restaurants offering movie and meal tickets are particularly suited.

Movie audiences tend to be in the 15–35 year age group. If your target market (your potential customers) are in this age bracket your business may benefit from cinema advertising.

Another way to promote your business with the cinema is to host the premiere of a new movie. Your company purchases the rights to this movie and you can invite as many people to the launch as will physically fit into the cinema. I remember being invited to a premiere of the movie *Arachnophobia* by a local pest control firm several years ago. They had their banners all over the cinema and they handed out flyers to people on the way out. This is a great way to reach about 400 people and enjoy some great word-of-mouth advertising.

Why not call your local cinema to see if they offer similar promotions?

56 Making a cheap television commercial that works

Television advertising can be expensive but of all the major mediums it can produce the best results in a very short amount of time. We have produced television commercials that have cost $75 000 and some that have cost $200. Both have very different applications but both have been equally successful.

The key to success with television advertising is producing a good commercial and placing advertisements in quality time slots. The most important point to remember is to decide what message you want to get across and stick to it. Too many companies try to say too much, leaving the customers confused about what they should do next. People tend to switch off and ignore poor advertisements.

Some of the key points to consider when producing an effective low-budget television commercial include:

- Plan the commercial to run like a story. Have a start and a finish.
- Decide on three or four key points that you want to get across.
- Try to be humorous. Cheap advertisements are OK if they are funny.
- Make sure people know where to find your business.
- Tell the people watching your commercial why they should buy something from your business.
- Test the commercial before airing it by showing it to friends and colleagues.
- Accept the fact that some people should never stand in front of a camera.

Television stations have all the necessary staff to help you produce your own advertisement. However, it has been my experience that you will have much greater success if you have a rough idea of what you want before you get started.

Once you have paid for your television commercial you own it. You can take a copy and play it on any television station you like. This policy may vary from station to station so make certain it is clarified beforehand.

Television commercials do have a limited life. While it would be ideal to make a new one every few months, very few businesses could afford to do this. Look at having a maximum shelf life of 12–18 months for your advertisement. Any longer than this and you will actually be doing your business more harm than good.

When it comes to placing your commercials, the important point to remember is to air them as often as you can afford in a short burst. What this means is that it is better for your commercial to be aired seven times in one night than once every day for seven days. This is called frequency.

Television commercials work because of their repetitive value. You can often negotiate with television stations for special rates. Remember that you will pay more for commercials aired during popular television programs but you will also reach a much greater number of viewers.

Television advertising can produce great results but if you haven't got enough money to make a good commercial and to air it often enough for people to notice, forget about it and move on to other ideas.

57 Bus advertising—inside and out

Advertising on buses is very popular, especially in major cities. Most advertisers are large national companies and government bodies. Research shows that this type of high-profile advertising is very effective and, in following with our principle of 'if it's good enough for big companies it's good enough for us', consider it as an option.

The advantage of bus advertising is that your sign is seen over large geographical areas. Most companies conducting a bus advertising campaign book 50 or 100 buses to saturate a particular area with their company slogan. In smaller regions the same effect can be reached by advertising on one or two buses.

With advancements in sign-making technology, cheap photographic quality signs can be produced for several hundred dollars.

Not all bus companies want advertising on their vehicles. The only way to really find out is to give them a call. Smaller regional bus companies are normally quite receptive to the concept as it helps to increase their bottom line profits without any outlay of revenue. Make sure that the buses are in good condition—a nice sign on a rusty old bus will not be complementary to your business.

Another point to remember is that signs on buses will generally be moving, making it quite difficult for people to read. Keep your words to a minimum, make it colourful and, if possible, make it funny.

Many bus companies also offer advertising inside their vehicles. This is an effective way to reach a particular audience. It is very important to ensure that the audience you will reach are the ones you want. If the bus company predominantly carries school children, are they your potential customers? The individual bus companies can provide you with these details.

58 Booking quality television, newspaper and radio advertising space

Booking quality advertising space is an art that many people specialise in. There are companies established that do nothing but book media. If you go to the expense and the time to produce advertisements, it is critical that you show them to the public in a way that will bring you the best results. I often see businesses spend months producing a television commercial that ends up being aired to three people at 2 a.m. Why bother?

Whenever you book any television, newspaper or radio advertising you will normally deal with a sales representative from the company. It is a good idea to strike up a good relationship with these people as they can really help your business.

Sometimes small business operators tend to feel that because they only book a small amount of media they are not as important as larger companies. This is not true and it is a part of the 'small business syndrome' discussed in the introduction of this book.

The main aim when booking media is to get the best results for the money you intend to spend. For this reason it is important that your media representative really makes an effort to provide you with the best possible schedule (a proposal for the placing of your advertisements) for your business. If you feel that the representative you have is not looking after your best interests, ring the company and request another rep. This may be harsh, but the success of your business is at stake. If they recommend a schedule and it doesn't work, they still get paid but you may not.

The first question that any media sales representative should ask you is, 'Who are you trying to reach?' This simply means who are your potential customers? If they are not asking you questions along those lines, how can they possibly book media that will reach your customers?

The second question they should ask you is about your budget. They are not trying to be nosy but they will need this information to plan a schedule.

Finally, they should follow up after the advertisements have run to see how they have gone. As you have been monitoring the results you can tell them. Be honest and don't try to downplay the success or failure of the campaign. The more honest you are with your representative the better equipped they will be to provide positive suggestions for your television, newspaper and radio advertisements.

Don't be pressured into buying more advertising than you can afford and always remember to book your spaces to reach your targeted audience.

59 Use cheap classified advertisements to generate business

Classified advertisements are relatively inexpensive. For a minimal cost you can have a couple of lines and a phone number in a column that will be read by people who have an interest in your product or service.

A local courier company advertises the fact that they will move furniture and fridges in the Garage Sales section of the classified advertisements. They get 3–4 phone calls per week that normally turn into jobs of about $20 in value. Now this may not sound like a lot but the advertisement costs $6 per week (it is only in the Saturday paper) and it generates between $60 and $80 worth of business.

In reality there are very few ways to advertise a business that can offer such a high return on your advertising outlay.

Mail-order businesses in particular focus on teaser advertisements in the classified section to generate leads. Limousine companies can advertise in the engagement section, funeral directors in the deaths column.

Think about a classified section that your particular business could take advantage of and advertise today. Give it time to work and if you are not getting a response, change the wording of your advertisement. Persevere and you will reap the benefits.

60 Get your suppliers to assist with your advertising

Quite often wholesale suppliers will assist with your advertising if it features their product. Many businesses already take full advantage of this, however, many do not. Most wholesalers have excellent high gloss brochures, sample radio advertisements, television footage, photographs and slides that you can use to promote your business and their products.

Ask the question. Contact your supplier and tell them that you would like to do some advertising. Ask them their policy regarding advertising. Most larger companies will have a standard policy and they may ask you to forward a prospectus.

We recently produced a magazine for a motorcycle club convention. Over 2500 members were attending the convention and the souvenir magazine was the main source of information providing valuable details about where the delegates had to be and when. This 38-page full colour magazine was paid for by advertising from motorcycle manufacturers and tour operators. The motorcycle club had a great souvenir for the event at no cost to the club and the advertisers had the opportunity to promote their businesses to the delegates. Everyone was happy.

61 Tap into large membership-based organisations

What is a large membership-based organisation? It is an organisation that people join to receive certain benefits. Auto clubs, unions and sports clubs are just a few examples.

One of the best known organisations is DEFCOM. DEFCOM is an organisation that has created a club for members of the defence force in Australia. This enables them to receive discounts at thousands of businesses Australia-wide. There are almost 100 000 DEFCOM members in Australia. Most countries around the world would have similar organisations.

DEFCOM produces publications where you can advertise your business. Most companies offer a discount of some sort as an added incentive for DEFCOM members. The sheer size of DEFCOM means that your results can be very good for a fairly minimal outlay. To find out more simply look up DEFCOM in the phone book.

Offering discounts to the various club members normally only requires doing some research and perhaps taking an advertisement in a club publication. This principle can be applied to local councils, large companies, schools and universities.

It is often surprising how receptive large organisations will be when small business operators call them for assistance with marketing ideas. How many larger organisations are there in your city that could be utilised to promote your business?

62 Making a radio advertisement that works

Radio advertising can be very effective as well as very affordable. Consider the idea of having your own business jingle made up. I used to always believe that this would cost thousands and thousands of dollars, but it does not. There are a lot of companies that make jingles all day every day and the prices can be as low as a few hundred dollars. You can end up with a catchy tune that portrays your business in a very professional manner and gives potential customers the feeling that if this business can afford their own jingle they must be reputable.

Just because someone can sing a catchy tune about a business does not guarantee the fact that they can do what they promise. It does, however, add to your overall corporate image and ultimately increases awareness of your business.

The following list identifies some of the tips for making a successful radio advertisement:

1. try to make the advertisement stand out from the crowd;
2. use humour wherever possible;
3. only try to get one point across in each radio advertisement;
4. repeat your point as many times as possible;
5. give the listener a reason to buy your product;
6. tell the listener when they should act; and
7. make sure the voices being used are good radio voices.

The radio station will help you produce your radio commercial. Once you pay for it you own it so you can take it away and play it on any other radio station you like. This policy may vary from station to station so make certain it is clarified beforehand.

Like most forms of media, you pay more for prime positions and it is important to decide exactly what your objectives are before booking air time. An advertisement that is played during prime time may have five times the number of people listening than at two in the morning, but you will probably pay five times the amount for that particular space.

Think about who you are trying to reach by advertising on the radio. If you are targeting pensioners, will they be listening at 2 a.m.? It is very unlikely; however, if you are targeting taxi drivers or shift workers, a 2 a.m. space is probably perfect.

Once you know who you are targeting and you have an idea when they will be listening (the radio station should be able to provide these figures) you can book your air time.

If you book 'run of station' for blanket coverage, the radio station will slot your advertisements in anywhere, normally with a proportionate mix of prime time and quiet time. This is the easiest way to book space; however, you really need to think long and hard about the benefits of your advertisements being played in the middle of the night.

Zone buys are also available. The day is divided into three time zones and you purchase advertising within a particular zone. This is cheaper than booking time during a specific program. Each radio station may offer a slight variation on this theme, making it worthwhile to discuss this concept with your sales representative.

Another option is to sponsor a regular radio feature like the weather or the drive time traffic report or the entertainment guide. If your business is relevant to an area like this, ask for prices on sponsoring that space.

63 Free local newspapers can produce plenty of work

Community newspapers offer an excellent way to advertise your business and their rates are normally much less than the commercial daily papers. Community papers are normally delivered free of charge once per week and the information contained in them focuses on local issues of importance.

Many smaller businesses tend to advertise in community papers, which really do offer a great medium for a business to get its message to potential customers living in the immediate area. Local traders and services in particular seem well suited for advertising in these publications.

Because of their nature, community newspapers are continually looking for events of particular relevance to the local community. If your business has something to contribute you can normally receive some excellent exposure free of charge. If you are having an event or sponsoring a competition, running a special offer to locals or introducing a new product or service to an existing business, let the paper know and they may do a feature.

Quite often you can include a flyer promoting your business as an insert in these newspapers. Of course, there is a charge associated with this but it is normally quite affordable and it can be very effective.

Advertising in television guides that are inserted in newspapers is another potential source of generating business. Results can be mixed but, like most advertising, the better the advertisement the better the results.

64 **Everyone gets one of these at the supermarket**

Advertising on the back of shopping dockets is not cheap but it can prove to be effective for certain businesses. A typical campaign will run for about twelve weeks. During this time your advertisement will appear thousands of times at shopping centres of your choice.

Next time you get a receipt start to take note of the type of companies that are advertising. You may be surprised to see some large national companies promoting special offers alongside the local takeaway food store.

From my experience, 'shop-a-dockets' work if your offer is good. Customers are spoiled by discounts and special offers, making it much harder to inspire the masses to buy your product if the offer is only mediocre. For example, anything less than 10 per cent and forget it. I often hear people saying they tried shop-a-dockets and they didn't work for them. Typically I ask what their offer was and, without exception, it is always a 5 per cent discount or something equally as insignificant.

I was once involved in a shop-a-docket campaign for a cruise ship operator that specialised in taking people to the Great Barrier Reef. The offer was sensational—two for the price of one. The ticket price was $98 so it represented a great saving for the local customers. This promotion was run at a time when the company was new, it was outside of the tourism season and the boat was running virtually empty. The $49 that we were getting from each of the shop-a-docket customers more than covered costs. The goodwill created was excellent and the company soon developed a solid reputation among the local residents. The campaign ran for about six months and several thousand dockets were redeemed.

The company has not repeated the promotion because it hasn't needed to. The main reason for the success of the promotion was the fact that it was a good offer.

If the cost is a bit scary, why not try doing the same thing on a smaller scale. Approach your local shop and sponsor their receipt rolls. Most printers will be able to print your company message on a roll to suit the cash register. You get great advertising and the shop owner gets free cash register rolls and perhaps a few dollars in their pocket.

65 If you are going to offer a discount, make it a good one

Discount coupons are rapidly becoming a way of life. In America it is a long-standing joke that nobody pays retail. Every time you turn around somebody is giving you a coupon of some description as an incentive to buy their product.

This trend is increasing and in all likelihood it will continue to grow in popularity simply because consumers love a bargain.

Like shop-a-dockets, the success of discount coupons depends on the offer you are making. If your proposed discount is less than 10 per cent your response will be minimal. Another option is to value-add the offer; for example, buy one get one free. Another option is to promote a price for an item and use that as the promotion; for example, developing films—36 exposures for $6.99. The normal price is not mentioned, neither is the percentage discount.

Be imaginative when participating in discount coupons. If one offer does not appear to get results, try varying the offer or the discount or the value-added option.

Marketing is about continually trying new ideas and refining ideas. If you hit upon something that works, keep using it until it stops working. Be patient with discount coupons. Do not expect thousands of people to come rushing in overnight—for some reason it takes time for the coupons to filter through to the community.

Many small business operators use cut-out coupons in their newspaper advertising. This can be very effective as long as the advertisement is easy to read and uncluttered. Is the offer good enough for someone to take the time to dig out the scissors and cut the coupon out? Restaurants in particular tend to take advantage of this type of coupon advertisement, but it could work equally as successfully for many other types of small business.

66 The perfect way to target families living in your area

School newsletters can be a cheap way to reach families living in your community. Quite often schools are happy to let local businesses advertise in their newsletters for a minimal cost. It helps to offset the production cost of the newsletter, enabling the school to spend the money in other areas.

Most schools have a minimum of several hundred students and many have several thousand. This represents a lot of households and families.

Some examples of businesses that could do this kind of promotion include:

- the local tyre company can advertise a reminder and special offer to check your tyres before going on school holidays;
- a driving school can target hundreds of potential customers as teenagers reach driving age;
- the local theme park can make special school holiday offers to keep the kids entertained;
- the toy store can have a school holiday special; and
- restaurants can offer a family special.

Obviously this type of promotion may not apply to every business but it does apply to most. If your local school doesn't have a regular newsletter perhaps you can encourage them to do one and your business can sponsor it.

67 Sponsor a courier and be seen all over town

Couriers travel all over town, visiting hundreds of businesses and potential customers every week. Offer to sponsor your local courier in return for some signage on their van, bike or on items like their clipboard, helmet, shirt or trousers.

The price for this is negotiable. Next time your courier comes in have a talk to them about the idea. If they received a few dollars per week or a new helmet once a year in return for some advertising they would more than likely jump at the offer.

Some businesses would be better suited than others to promote in this way. For example, a bike shop would get great exposure by sponsoring a bike courier, perhaps a stationery shop for the clipboard or a uniform supplier for the shirt. The potential is unlimited and the exposure for your business could be considerable. Sponsoring a courier is like sponsoring a Grand Prix racing car, only on a smaller scale.

A number of clever business operators have developed a very high-profile way to promote their business. Basically they find someone with a big truck and they paint a company advertisement down the side. The effects of this are very visual.

First, it looks like the truck actually belongs to the company doing the advertising, which makes them appear very large and successful, ultimately giving the business a good deal of credibility. The second benefit is that the advertisement will be seen by thousands of other motorists travelling on the same roads as the truck, resulting in some very effective advertising.

The hard part is probably finding a truck for you to advertise on. If your company moves a lot of freight with one particular company, they may be prepared to let you paint up one of their vehicles. Many large national companies have this as part of their freight contract. In return for the business they must be allowed to paint a certain number of trucks with their company advertising.

Another option is to approach an owner-operator and offer to pay some of their costs, such as registration or insurance for the year, in return for you putting an advertisement on their truck.

68 Advertise your business from behind

Four-wheel drive spare tyre covers are relatively inexpensive. They are found on the back of the vehicle and they are the perfect place for your company message to be proudly displayed. If you are not sure where to get these covers, call your local recreational off-road specialist store. Most sign-writers will paint your message directly onto the cover.

Perhaps some of your friends or staff may be willing to promote your company message in return for the wheel cover. If the answer is yes, you could end up having mobile signs being seen all day long throughout the entire city.

Design the wheel cover to be simple, easy to read, and make sure that you remember to include your telephone number. It is also good to remember that you are benefiting from the advertising so remember to be grateful to any staff member or customers who are willing to promote your business in this manner.

A new material that has recently become available can be used to put a sign in your car's back window. This sign is completely transparent when looking from inside the car but to people looking in it is bright and colourful and very easy to read. Taxis are advertising various products and services with these signs.

Most sign-writers would be aware of this new material and it could easily be used on any company vehicle as another way to promote your business from behind.

69 Inserting promotional material in newspapers

Inserting your promotional material in newspapers and magazines is an alternative to advertising in these publications. You can insert anything from a newsletter to a brochure to a business card. Most newspapers are happy to take inserts, generally charging a fixed price per thousand. If you inserted a brochure into every copy of the publication it would cost you a lot more than placing an advertisement. However, the joy of inserts is that you can do them to suit your budget or, in the case of letterbox-dropped publications, you can choose the geographical area that you would like covered.

Putting promotional material in papers is an alternative to straight letterbox drops, and many marketing people argue that it is better to have your material in a local paper rather than by itself in a letterbox as most junk mail goes in the bin whereas people tend to read local papers. Another advantage of putting a brochure in the local paper is that it will get wrapped up if the weather is wet. If you just drop a flyer in a letterbox the odds are that it will get destroyed as soon as it rains. Of course, you pay for this service, hence inserts cost more than letterbox drops.

Local newspapers can also be put into letterboxes that have 'no junk mail' signs on them. So if your material is inside the paper you have managed to get inside a house where a normal letterbox drop would not.

A point to remember is that if you fail to get a response to the insert don't immediately blame the paper they were delivered in because, odds-on, the problem is your promotional material. I tend to suggest creating a brochure or flyer specifically designed to be inserted in a newspaper. Try and keep to a simple formula with big bold headings, clear easy-to-read text, a picture of the product and a few testimonials from satisfied customers if possible.

As always, keep your eyes open for inserts in newspapers that have impressed you. Try to identify what caught your eye and see if you can imitate the same qualities when promoting your own business in this manner.

10 | Does your business have credibility?

Having credibility is an important factor in giving your customers confidence in your products. We are all concerned about being ripped off by unethical business operators. There are many things that you can do to ensure that your business does have credibility and they are detailed in this section:

#70   Offer a 100 per cent money back guarantee
#71   Get behind organisations that support the community
#72   Don't underestimate the intelligence of your customers
#73   Support a local team—a small cost for great exposure
#74   Scan the newspaper for goodwill opportunities

70 Offer a 100 per cent money back guarantee

This is a major selling point that most businesses are too scared to offer because they have visions of hundreds of customers running back and asking for a refund. Offering a 100 per cent money back guarantee means that you believe in your product so much that if a customer isn't satisfied you will gladly give them their money back.

Who wouldn't be happy with this type of offer? It helps take the pressure and the risk out of a purchase. When you buy the product you know that if it's not exactly what you wanted you can take it back and get your refund.

Research shows that the percentage of people who return products is very small and in most cases the reason for the return is very legitimate.

Offer an unconditional guarantee in your business and you will see the results. Use the slogan in your advertising and on your flyers and, most importantly, believe in your product enough to offer this kind of guarantee. Also remember that if someone does come back to you for a refund, hand it over gladly with a minimum of fuss and you will probably keep the customer coming back.

In general, customer complaints are handled very poorly. See how most large department stores handle customer returns—goods are exchanged or refunds issued on the spot, no questions and no exceptions, and the customers keep coming back. They understand that if you handle a complaint well the customers will continue to use your business.

Most smaller businesses take complaints personally. Get over it—we all make mistakes but the winners learn how to handle them quickly, efficiently and politely and they keep in mind that the customer is always right. If someone has a fair complaint and they want a refund, don't argue with them, give them their refund and move on.

71 Get behind organisations that support the community

Being an active member of the community can only help your business. Most successful people I know gladly give their time and expertise to helping others and the community in general. There is a spin-off in doing this and that is that people in turn will support you.

Most community organisations are formed by business leaders within the community. This provides an excellent opportunity to meet some very influential decision-makers. I am not suggesting that you join community organisations simply to get more business. I am saying that if you join a community organisation and lend a hand, your reward will come in the form of business.

There are a number of community projects with no budget that need assistance. Perhaps your input can help a project to become a reality, which would make you feel good about yourself and help others less fortunate. As with all positive attitude-type action, make sure that your motivation is doing the right thing, not the financial reward.

Our company gets behind one or two charities or events each year and we offer to market and publicise them free of charge. We love doing it and, once again, everyone wins.

This is probably a little off the wall for some entrepreneurs. However, I firmly believe that good deeds are rewarded. Call it karma, call it divine intervention, call it what you like, but from my experience those people that do the right thing, have good business ethics and are honest and kind seem to have successful businesses.

I can't explain why or how, I can only say that it is an observation I have made—those people that sit behind the counter with a face like a prune and a bad attitude generally have suffering businesses. Make the effort, do a few nice things for people every once in a while. The worst that can happen is that your business will grow.

I know a few companies that are always there when a house burns down to give the victims a free television or a new refrigerator or a holiday or a computer—I shop at these companies because I think the people running them are generous people.

One point though—if you are going to be kind and generous do it sincerely, not just as a marketing ploy. People trust genuine people. If your customers are aware of your contribution to the community it will only increase the faith and trust they have when frequenting your business.

72 Don't underestimate the intelligence of your customers

This is a mistake that I see some businesses making on a regular basis. They tend to assume that their customers are stupid. I think this is a very dangerous assumption to make. After all, we are all consumers and I don't know about you but I certainly don't feel stupid.

Some business operators tend to feel they can say anything or make any offer and their customers will come running in the door. That may have been the case a few years ago but now competition is increasing so dramatically that the consumers have the upper hand.

People spend a lot of time shopping and buying things in general. They know that certain stores have sales on a regular basis and some places are more expensive than others. They also know that if they don't get what they want from one particular business they can take their credit card and go somewhere else.

I believe you should consider customers to be identical to you. How do you like to be treated? What type of discount do you look for when you are bargain hunting? How do you want to be treated if you have a complaint? One of the best ways to upset a customer is to sell them something at full price the day before your 30 per cent storewide sale. We have all experienced this and I don't know about you but I find it very frustrating.

If you find that your business has developed an almost cynical approach to the customers that pay your bills, maybe it is time to rethink your business philosophy. Even if you have the right attitude, make sure that staff appreciate both the intelligence and the importance of your customers.

73 Support a local team—a small cost for great exposure

Every major sporting team around the world has at least one giant corporation sponsoring them. Yet again, let's bring this down to a smaller, more affordable level and look at sponsoring a local team.

When you get down to children's teams, sponsorship normally means providing the team with shirts and maybe some sporting equipment. This is not an expensive exercise. Think about the exposure your business will receive—first, the team members and their immediate families and supporters will look more favourably upon your business, then members of the local community will perhaps read snippets about your team in the newspaper or see them on the television. Every time they play a game your business gets the exposure.

Often sporting teams adopt the name of the major sponsor and the same principle can be used for your business sponsorship.

Another benefit of sponsorship like this is that you are putting something back into the community where you live and work and that is a good thing. All of this for a few hundred dollars. To me that is a bargain.

An extension of this idea is signage at the grounds of local sports parks. Approach any sporting venue and enquire about signage. It can be inexpensive and as long as you get a good sign-writer to make up the sign, the effect can be very professional.

I observed an example of how this can work at a recently opened go-kart track. This sport has a large world following and international events can host thousands of people. Signage was available at the local track for $200 per year. You would have to agree that this is a cheap form of marketing, especially for international exposure.

Sporting clubs and venues are normally very happy to talk about signage as it is a means of creating extra income at no real expense to them.

Remember that this is an excellent way to target the people living in your community.

74 Scan the newspaper for goodwill opportunities

Every day we read hard luck stories in the newspaper or hear them on the radio or evening news about people who are sick, a family in crisis, a business crisis, a house burnt down, victims of crime and so on.

These stories are often very sad and touch most. An effective way to do some good and to receive some free publicity is to offer to help people in unfortunate situations in any way that your business can.

Recently there was a shocking story about a dog on the front page of the paper. This dog had been abandoned and left tied to a shed for weeks. It was literally nothing but skin and bone. I couldn't look at the picture without feeling ill.

The RSPCA felt the dog would need to be put down fairly quickly as it was very ill. The next day the local vet rang the RSPCA and adopted the dog. They were going to do everything in their power to help this animal survive and they did.

Every week the newspaper ran an article to show the progress of the dog, which was nothing short of a miracle. The vet clinic was inundated with money, cards, faxes, phone calls and letters of encouragement for their deed. Instead of accepting gifts they asked people to send a donation to the RSPCA.

The dog has recovered and, once again, everyone wins. I think this vet deserves to have a very successful practice and I am sure he does.

11 | Are you willing to go out and chase business?

While many marketing ideas are relatively passive, meaning you implement them and then sit back and watch for results, there are many others that are more aggressive. These involve taking your message to the customer and actually chasing the business. The ideas discussed in this section look at ways for you to take a more active role in marketing your business. They include:

#75   Doing your first letterbox drop

#76   Use local markets to promote your business

#77   Talk to your neighbours

#78   Commit to making ten phone calls every day

#79   Always try to sell to the decision-maker, not their assistant

#80   Using the facsimile to sell directly to other businesses

#81   Always make a follow-up call after the sale

#82   Tips for making a good sales presentation

#83   What is 'direct mail' and can you use it?

#84   Take your message to the streets

#85   Put your brochure in government and corporate mail-outs

#86   Don't underestimate the value of trade shows and expos

#87   Do a combined mail-out with other businesses

#88   Run free training seminars

75 Doing your first letterbox drop

Letterbox drops can be a very effective and economical way to canvass potential customers in your area. As always, when you rummage through today's junk mail, look at the big name corporations that have decided you need to see their catalogues. If it's good enough for them it's good enough for you.

To do a letterbox drop all you really need is a flyer of some sort, photocopied in lots of a thousand. I prefer an A5 size for flyers, which is an A4 normal sheet of paper folded in half. To get a thousand of these flyers you will need to get 500 pages photocopied at about 5 cents per page—making a cost of about $25.

The next thing you need is a good pair of walking shoes, a bag of some sort and maybe a map. Now the marketing campaign can begin. You may want to start with the houses close to your business and slowly move further afield.

If you want to cover a lot more area, you may require the services of professional letterbox droppers. Professional letterbox drop companies charge per thousand and it is normally only a minimal charge. You can normally choose which areas you would like covered. You can find the companies that do letterbox deliveries in the Yellow Pages (under letterbox).

It is always a good idea to do a few test drops first of all to make certain your promotional material works. Make up a number of flyers with different headings. Pick a suburb, have a letterbox drop and then monitor the results. Repeat this exercise in several suburbs and see which flyer produces the best results and then do a mass letterbox drop. The overall response will be much higher if you adopt this method of trial and error on a small scale first and then go for a larger-scale mass mail-out once you have ironed out the bugs.

Once again, do as many households as you can afford. Better to spend $65 to do one thousand households once per month than to do none at all. Believe it or not, a good response is 2–3 per cent from a direct-mail campaign (that's 20–30 responses per thousand).

76 Use local markets to promote your business

Market stalls are a great way to promote your business. A stall at most markets costs very little. Good markets attract thousands of people so why not set up a booth to promote you and your business?

Perhaps a vet could set up a booth themed along the lines of pet care. Brochures can be handed out detailing how to look after your pets and new products available, and pet training books and various other products could be sold.

Another good idea is to run a competition. The vet could offer a free check-up for the family pet as the prize. To enter, simply fill in the form and drop it in the box. The vet then ends up with a huge database of people that live in their area and have pets. This list can be used for direct mail-outs at a later date.

Perhaps a mechanic could set up a booth to answer questions people have about their vehicles—it is very likely they will receive some business from the people they talk to.

Like most marketing, the aim is to get your message across to as many potential customers as possible for the minimum cost. Markets provide one of the best ways known to target a large number of people for very little outlay. Consider this next time you have a free Saturday morning.

77 Talk to your neighbours

I was recently visiting a client in a major shopping centre when two tourists walked into the shop and asked the owner for a recommendation for a restaurant for lunch. The owner asked a few questions and determined that the tourists were looking for a seafood meal in a restaurant with a nice view.

I was somewhat surprised when my client started to explain how to get to a restaurant about 15 minutes' walk away, outside the centre. After the people left I asked why she hadn't recommended the seafood restaurant overlooking a magnificent marina inside the actual centre. Her answer was simply that she didn't even know there was a restaurant there.

I have noticed this phenomenon a lot. Businesses are not aware of what their neighbours actually do. Very rarely do people take the time to pop next door and ask the neighbour exactly what services they offer.

I did this at my office recently and picked up two small projects worth about $3000 simply because I took two minutes to introduce myself to my neighbours. One company needed a brochure made up and the other needed a marketing strategy for a new product they had developed.

How aware are you of the services your neighbours offer? More importantly, do you recommend them if people ask you and, even more importantly again, do they recommend you? The potential for that extra business we all need could be a few doors away. Take a moment and introduce yourself to the neighbours.

78 **Commit to making ten phone calls every day**

Most successful marketing professionals realise that a lot of their success is due to simple perseverance and always having a prospective sale on the horizon. The big question is how do they always manage to have a prospective customer on the horizon? The answer is simple—contact a lot of people.

If you make ten phone calls per day to either prospective clients or even current clients you will have made 50 contacts that week, 200 for the month and 2400 for the year.

For the current clients it is good after-sales service to follow-up with a call, say thank you for the business and perhaps ask for a testimonial or a referral. For the new customer, every call you make is putting you one step closer to getting their business. If you are not sure who to call, start by using the Yellow Pages as a way of finding companies that may be able to utilise your product. Given time you will always find prospective clients.

If you have run a competition you might have several hundred entries that you can follow up with a phone call.

However, if you plan to utilise this marketing tool, make it a habit. Every day religiously make contact with ten people. Determine whether that mix will be five existing customers and five potential customers or a mix slightly different to suit your current business needs. Every call that you make is either sourcing new business or reinforcing existing business.

79 Always try to sell to the decision-maker, not their assistant

If you are trying to target a specific company always try to contact the decision-maker or the person who signs the cheque. From my experience, if I can see the decision-maker I can sell the product. If I have to go through the pecking order the sale is often lost in the system.

The reason for this is clear. If I can present my product to the decision-maker, I know that they have one major concern—the bottom line. If the product that I am selling is going to increase their bottom line, they will buy it.

I have lost track of the number of times I have met a decision-maker at a social function of some sort, shown them a product (that I always carry), they have said it was great and it is exactly the type of thing their business could use. Then I have to tell them that I have already shown it to the purchasing officer and they told me to go away. Without fail I get the 'drop by tomorrow morning' and they sign up on the spot.

If you cannot get past one person you may be obliged to wait for that person to leave the company (which happens a lot quicker these days). Patience is a real virtue when it comes to any form of selling. If you persevere you will eventually get the client. The difference between success and failure is normally only a matter of time.

80 Using the facsimile to sell directly to other businesses

The facsimile is an excellent way to spread your message. We are all conditioned to believe that any message that comes across the facsimile is important. Do you race over to check it out as soon as the machine rings?

Make up a simple flyer or perhaps you can fax through your company brochure. Make sure that whatever you are sending is easy to read and be certain that it will fax clearly (either fax a copy to a friend or copy the flyer first just to make certain). There is nothing worse than getting a 30-page facsimile or one that you cannot read.

Use the facsimile to tell the world about your business, coming specials and new products. The next time you are sitting behind the counter and things are quiet, get on the fax machine and go crazy. For a few dollars you can fax a lot of people and the response to fax campaigns can be quite high.

There are books available that are pre-made funny faxes you can use. Andrew Matthews produces the best. We use these funny faxes to collect overdue accounts and to try and get people's attention. Without fail they work.

Faxes are quick, easy and non-threatening, making them an excellent marketing tool.

81 Always make a follow-up call after the sale

Another common mistake is forgetting the customer once they walk out the door. All it takes is a simple telephone call. Are you happy with the product, was our service good, is there anything else that we can do to help, do you mind if we drop you a line from time to time to let you know what new products we have available?

How many companies ring you to see if you are happy with your purchase? I have spent over $20 000 on computer equipment from the one store in the past three years and I have never once received a follow-up call to see how it is all going. Admittedly they are a very busy store but I can't help but wonder how many more software packages and optional pieces of equipment they would sell if they rang me two to three weeks after selling me a computer. By this time I have it installed, have most glitches worked out and now I am ready for work. If someone rang and said that you could easily attach a 'bingpop' to that system and you would be able to email everyone in the world for only $500, I would probably buy it.

But they never ring. In fact, only two companies have ever rung. One was a caryard ringing to ask how the new car was going and reminding me that the first 1000 kilometres service was critical (and free). The second company that regularly does after-sales calls is, once again, our laser printer cartridge supplier. Did you get the last cartridge, is it OK, did it take long to arrive, would you like us to call in a few weeks for your next order and so on?

Both of these companies are very smart. From a customer's point of view, how could you not be impressed? The other nice thing is that their phone call is not trying to sell me something—it is a genuine check to see how things are going, but I nearly always buy something anyway.

Very few businesses do this kind of after-sales follow-up call. If you are one that doesn't, perhaps you can increase business simply by making an after-sales follow-up call.

82 Tips for making a good sales presentation

There is no doubt there are very few methods of advertising as effective as calling on someone directly. This generally means making an appointment and going to visit a prospective client. For many people this is an everyday occurrence but for others it is unheard of and, in reality, quite daunting.

Perhaps your business could benefit from you making the effort to call on one prospective customer per day. Obviously the more the better but, like all marketing, start small and work your way up. This is one area that larger companies tend to fall down in. They are trying to reach such large markets that they have to use mass marketing measures like television and newspaper.

Over the years I have written millions of dollars worth of business by doing direct sales calls. Sometimes for employers and sometimes in my own businesses. The situation doesn't matter, neither does the type of business you operate. A prospective customer appreciates you making the effort and if you look after them they will reward you with loyal business for a long time.

There are of course a few important protocols you should follow when making a direct sales call. Follow these, be patient and you will be amazed at the results. Remember there are thousands of books written on this subject, so if you feel that you would like to pursue this form of marketing, spend a few dollars and invest in some. The best sales book that I have ever read was written by Dale Carnegie in 1953, called *How to win friends and influence people*. The title is terrible but the book is fantastic. If you look on the shelves or in the drawers of any top performing salespeople you can rest assured that there is a copy of this book close by (a recommended reading list can be found in the Appendix of this book).

A few points to remember when making sales calls:

1. Find out a bit about the person or company that you are targeting.
2. Make sure that you are talking to the person who makes the buying decision.
3. Make an appointment.
4. Arrive on time, neatly dressed and be organised.
5. Look around the office or building for anything of interest that you could start a conversation with.
6. Have a few minutes of small talk and thank the person for seeing you.
7. Explain why you are there.
8. Ask them about their business and their requirements.
9. Outline your product or service (in a few minutes) based on their needs.
10. Ask for the person's thoughts or questions.
11. Don't be afraid to ask for the business.
12. If they ask you for more information get it to them quickly and call to make sure they received it.

Point number 11 is probably the most important but the least often done—asking for the business.

I have seen thousands of great presentations with bells and whistles, overhead projectors, laptop presentations, glossy brochures and high-tech videos but by far the most common fault that salespeople have is that they don't ask for the business, which is of course the whole reason they are there.

At the end of their presentation they pack up all of their gizmos and walk out the door without once ever asking the customer for the business.

By following the above suggestions you will dramatically increase your chances of conducting successful sales calls.

83 What is 'direct mail' and can you use it?

Direct mail is when you send someone a letter of some description encouraging them to buy your product. It is a very commonly used marketing tool and it is very popular with the larger companies.

Direct mail is a science. There are thousands of books written about it and it is accepted as a very effective way to sell a product. Research shows that over 130 million Americans have made purchases by direct mail. That is approximately half of the population.

Direct mail basically involves sending a person a catalogue or brochure about your products. The customer responds, normally paying by credit card. Examples of successful mail-order products include wine clubs, financial institutions (promoting credit cards), travel packages, clothing, books, magazine subscriptions, collectables (Franklin Mint), music and stationery.

The key to running a successful direct mail campaign is to get people to read your letter. In these modern times we all receive a lot of direct mail on a daily basis—if it looks like junk it goes straight in the bin. To overcome this try the following tips:

- personally address the envelope and the letter;
- handwrite the envelope;
- use an odd-sized envelope;
- include an easy response form (accepting all types of credit cards); and
- use an accurate database and make sure all contact details are correct.

A successful direct marketing campaign is one where you receive a 3–4 per cent response rate. So for every hundred letters sent out you are hoping for three or four people to buy your product. This is an important figure to remember because if you are selling a low-priced item you may struggle to make it profitable.

The best advice is to buy a book that specialises in direct mail (there are hundreds) and follow the step-by-step guides. Direct mail works very well—take the time to learn about it and your business will receive the benefits.

84 Take your message to the streets

Handing out flyers can be very profitable and I know a lot of businesses that swear by this marketing method. One in particular is a restaurant in a high-profile shopping centre. This restaurant employs a promotional person seven days per week to walk through the centre handing out flyers. Their figures show that business drops by 40 per cent if they do not hand out the flyers. This restaurant has almost 1000 customers per day so to lose 400 of them by not handing out flyers is unimaginable.

Like all promotional flyers they need to be simple to read, have a catchy heading and, best of all, a discount or special offer to really encourage the consumer to bring the flyer in to claim their free service or product.

Another form of joint promotion that has been used very successfully is to have one business promoting itself on one side of the flyer and another business on the other side. Both companies share the costs of distribution and production and they achieve the same results.

Handing out flyers can be very cost-effective if you find that you have staff standing around doing nothing a lot of the time but you are committed to having the staff numbers on hand. Keep them close to the store so that if things get busy or if another staff member needs a break they can be back in a couple of minutes.

If you are in charge of promotions and marketing for your business, hit the pavement yourself. Put flyers under the doors of businesses over the weekend. I have spent many a Saturday and Sunday doing this and the results are surprising. A little effort can have a big result.

Remember, the better your flyer the better your results will be.

85 Put your brochure in government and corporate mail-outs

Quite often large government organisations will let you include promotional material when they send out their bills, such as rates, registration renewals etc. In return for this you pay a small fee per letter.

This can be a very cost-effective way to do a mail-out to a large number of people. If you consider the cost of sitting down and doing a mail-out on your own, a conservative figure would be $1 per letter. When doing it cooperatively like this it can drop to 10 per cent of this amount.

Not all government departments and councils offer this service. However, as I always try to point out, there is nothing wrong with asking the question. Pick up the phone and call the local council. The worst that can happen is that they say no.

Many private companies that do large mail-outs on a regular basis are more than happy to offset their costs by including promotional material for other companies in their mail-outs.

86 Don't underestimate the value of trade shows and expos

I have attended a lot of trade shows during the past ten years. I believe that they are an exceptional way to find new business. There are basically two types of shows—one is for the trade, which means that members of a particular industry get together to showcase new products and technology in a trade show format. The other is open to the general public, normally known as an expo.

From my experience you only get results out of a trade show or expo if you put the effort in. Make your booth interesting, always have it staffed with professional people who can answer any question, ensure an adequate supply of brochures and promotional material and look for every opportunity to showcase your products and services.

I attended a travel show in Tasmania, Australia, several years ago. This show was open to the public and featured tourism operators from around the country. I was representing a Great Barrier Reef boating company, as was the gentleman in the booth next to my stand. I set my booth up with posters, displays of diving equipment and sunny pictures of the Great Barrier Reef. The chap next to me had a bare table with four enormous stacks of brochures. There were no other decorations and his booth looked disgraceful. Once the show opened the man running the booth hid behind the piles of brochures and chain-smoked cigarettes all day. The only time he left his booth on the first day was to go to the bar. On the second day he didn't even go to his booth and on the third morning he topped up the brochure piles and disappeared.

During that trip I was lucky enough to make contact with a gentleman who was taking 100 people to North Queensland in the near future—he booked a $200 per person package on the spot ($20 000 worth of business). There were countless other small groups and enquiries and in general it was a good show. The man in the booth next to me would report back that it was a waste of time—nothing but people taking brochures. I have never been to a trade show that was a waste of time.

I attended another trade show in Papua New Guinea. Everyone considered this a junket. During the show I was fortunate enough to have a booth next to the P&O Cruises representative. As we chatted he told me about an unscheduled stopover that the *Fairstar* was making in Cairns in 8 weeks.

On the spot I got the information, faxed a letter to their head office and received a booking for 270 people to travel out to the Great Barrier Reef with our company.

These examples are not meant to embellish my own sales ability. The point I am trying to make is that if you are serious about getting business from trade shows, don't consider them a hassle. Never send your most inexperienced staff member or juniors to work on the stand. If you own the business you should be there.

Run a competition, build up a database and follow up with the people that visit your booth. You may end up with hundreds of new customers for a small financial outlay. Research shows that a large proportion of leads are never followed up after trade shows. If you're not serious about business, why bother going?

87 Do a combined mail-out with other businesses

Bundling is basically where you and several other companies bundle your flyers and brochures together and then have them delivered as one package—normally by letterbox drop. The advantage of this is that your distribution costs are shared and there is more possibility of people reading a bundle of information rather than a single flyer.

One letterbox drop I regularly receive is called the Yellow Envelope. When you open it up there are about 30 company flyers, discount coupons, incentives etc. A lot of the information is applicable and relevant and usually a lot is junk.

If you have a few business associates you work well with, why not put your own bundling package together. For example, why not make up a 'Complete Car Care Package' with information from a car detailer, a mechanic, an auto parts store, a tyre shop, a car stereo shop and an insurance company. The same could be done for health care promotion, professional services, household services, garden services, business services and so on.

Think logically about exposing your business to as many potential customers as possible. The more cost-effectively you do this, the more customers you will be able to reach.

88 Run free training seminars

I recently saw an advertisement in the paper promoting a three-hour training seminar on car maintenance. The course was designed to teach basic car maintenance skills such as checking oil, water, tyre pressure, battery levels, automatic transmission fluids etc. The course was only available for women and it was free of charge. It was being run by the local caryard.

This is a very clever idea and the principle is applied in many other businesses. We often see free seminars about subjects such as creating wealth, investing, personal development, weight loss and other similar areas of interest. If the seminar is free, the odds are that the people running the seminar will want to sell you something. It might be a book, it might be a training program, a video or cassette tape.

A friend of mine wrote a book on weight loss. She published the book herself and promoted it through a series of free seminars entitled 'How to stop dieting and start living today'. Through these seminars she has sold over 5000 books in a few months.

The free seminar draws the crowd and enables the business to sell their product. Perhaps your business could run free seminars you could then use to sell your products.

Some other great free seminar ideas include a nursery running a course on landscaping or making beautiful potplants. The beautician running a seminar on looking your best for job interviews. The wedding caterer could run a seminar on planning a successful wedding. There are thousands of potential seminar topics and as long as you can run them for free you will draw a good crowd.

12 | Do you think like a customer?

This question may sound strange but do you think like a customer? It is amazing how different a business looks when you are viewing it from the customer's point of view. This change in perception is a worthy exercise that we all should do on a regular basis. The ideas mentioned in this section are designed to help you increase the appeal of your business to potential customers, and include:

#89   Use your waiting room or reception area to sell your services

#90   Always have a top quality window display to attract interest

#91   Ask your customers how they heard about your business

#92   Offering free delivery may give you the competitive edge

#93   Have ongoing quality SALES

#94   The power of free samples

#95   Offer a second opinion for free

#96   What is 'value adding' and can you use it?

#97   Using a 'gift with purchase' to sweeten the deal

89 Use your waiting room or reception area to sell your services

Getting people to walk in the front door of any business is a challenge, so once they are in you need to do as much as possible to promote your services to them and sell them on the fact that your company is going to meet and exceed their expectations.

I am often amazed at how poorly businesses promote themselves at their own premises. This is the perfect opportunity to tell a customer about some of the services your business offers, reinforcing the fact that you are a good company, reputable with plenty to offer.

Virtually all businesses that deal with the general public have an area where customers gather either to pay or to wait, such as cash registers at grocery stores. Look at the mass of material and products crowded around the registers waiting to be picked up by bored customers standing in line. Most waiting rooms are drab, poorly furnished and with little or no promotional material (let alone decent reading material).

My dentist has excellent promotional material showing all of the services the surgery offers. There are great photo albums of before and after treatments from teeth whitening to complete sets of false teeth.

If you have an area like this use it to your full advantage. Put up promotional material, specials, free samples, a corporate video playing on a television in the background or certificates awarded to your business. If you have letters from happy customers, frame them and put them on the wall. Use this area to sell yourself and reinforce the message that you are a reputable business.

Any staff in the waiting area should be trained to sell your services to waiting customers. Take a few minutes to have a look at your waiting room. I bet there are plenty of ways to promote your business in this area.

90 Always have a top quality window display to attract interest

I am constantly amazed when I walk past a shop window on a busy street and see a ramshackle, dusty and dingy window display that looks like it hasn't been changed in ten years. Customers will decide whether or not they should enter your store based upon your window display, making it crucial that you get it right.

If you want to see this principle working, find a pet shop with puppies and kittens in the window. They draw a crowd and the crowd moves into the shop. I have witnessed this phenomenon in pet shops around the world and it is universally successful.

If you are not certain how to go about making a good window display, do a bit of research. Grab your camera and visit some of the major department stores. These companies spend a lot of money getting the window displays right because they know how important they are. Find a few shops similar to yours and see what displays they have in their windows. Look for businesses that seem to be drawing a crowd and take a photo of their window displays.

A few common themes come out and they should be considered when planning your window display:

- change the display regularly;
- don't clutter the front window;
- use bright colours to attract attention and repaint the window box when you are changing displays;
- make sure that your window box has good lighting; and
- keep your windows clean.

Try not to look at changing window displays as a drudgery but rather as a key component to running your business. Get your suppliers to provide you with professional sales material; make the windows interesting and fun. Do whatever you can to catch people's eye and give them the feeling that they should look a little closer at your shop.

91 Ask your customers how they heard about your business

One of the most common remarks I hear from business people is that 'I tried advertising and it didn't work'. My response to this is always the same—how do you know it didn't work? The answer is that no one rang or sales did not increase on the day or something equally as vague. The only way to really determine where your customers have heard about you is to ask them. People are happy to answer this question and, in fact, most are quite impressed that you care enough to ask.

The only industry I have witnessed that truly embraces this principle is accounting. Recently I was looking for a new accountant. I received recommendations for six accounting firms from business associates and friends and I proceeded to make appointments to see each of them. During my meetings every firm asked me how I had heard about them—and I was glad to tell them.

If you know where your customers are finding out about your business you will soon know what marketing is working and what is not. Keep a note pad by the phone or cash register so that you can write down each and every response. Train your staff to ask the question and make sure that they get into the habit of writing the response down. If it is not recorded it is not accurate.

An interesting story that comes to mind is about an old client of mine. They ran a 'shop-a-docket' promotion where they offered a 50 per cent discount on admission to their tourist attraction. The promotion ran for twelve weeks. Halfway through the promotion they rang me to say that it was a complete waste of time and money and they were very disappointed—they said they had only collected five coupons. I was very surprised by this as I had used this form of advertising in a similar way in the past and it had worked very well.

A few days later I visited the business to talk to the owners. Unfortunately they were out. I needed to send a fax so one of the staff members led me to the office and sent the fax off for me. While I was waiting I dropped a pen which fell into a bin. When I retrieved the pen I saw a pile of 'shop-a-docket' coupons in the rubbish. The lady that had taken me into the office said that every morning after the manager had balanced the tills they threw the coupons in the bin because they were no longer needed. They estimated that they had thrown out over one thousand coupons in the past six weeks.

When I confronted the business owners about this they were very embarrassed. They had absolutely no idea that the coupons were being thrown away. On the cash register they were recorded as promotional discounts—one of hundreds they had in the marketplace with no way to be more specific on the origin of the coupons.

Needless to say, after a few operational changes this type of problem has been overcome. The main point I am trying to make is simply that you should not write off a promotion as being a failure unless you have all the facts.

Find out how your customers found out about your business and then do more of it.

92 Offering free delivery may give you the competitive edge

One of the critical factors in running a successful business is defining what makes you different from your competition. This is discussed in detail in the introduction of this book and it is the basic fundamental principle of a good business.

In this high-pressure, fast world, time is critical. If you can offer a customer free pick up or free drop off or both then you will have an advantage. Takeaway restaurants have learned the value of free delivery very quickly and in many cases consumers are more than happy to pay a few dollars extra to offset the costs. It is quick, it is convenient and it is easy.

Why should pizza shops be the only businesses to benefit from free delivery? Perhaps your business would benefit by offering this service. Exactly how much will it cost your business to offer free pick up or delivery? Couriers do local deliveries for only a few dollars each way. If you can absorb the costs, why not try it?

Imagine if there are two electrical appliance companies in the phone book. One offers free pick up and the other does not. Which one would you use? Imagine if you were an elderly person who found it difficult to get out, let alone carry the toaster to the repair shop. Imagine a vet that offered a free pick up and delivery service or a bait shop that delivered your prawns while you got the boat ready.

Like any extra service, it is only a benefit if you tell your customers that you offer it. Include your free delivery in all of your advertising and promotional material.

93 **Have ongoing quality SALES**

A phenomenon you may have noticed about some businesses is that they seem to always be having a special of some sort. They are closing down, they are having a birthday, they are moving, they are stocktaking and so on. Their year is really one big sale.

I am not suggesting this is the way you should run your business marketing activity, but I am suggesting that sales are a part of life and consumers not only like them but they expect them. All businesses can have specials and all businesses should have specials because they make customers feel lucky and they tend to buy more. Everyone enjoys a bargain and those businesses that are prepared to offer good deals tend to win. It is also the perfect way to move old stock.

A clever menswear shop in our local shopping centre always has two huge sales bins at the front of the shop. Most of the menswear stocked in the store is expensive but the discount bins are great buys and generally very good quality. The philosophy of the store owners is that the discount bins will bring people into the shop and get them into the buying mood. If they find a bargain, great; they may be happy to purchase another item at full price.

An important point to make here is that sales should be genuine sales—not just junk. Don't try and fool customers by off-loading trash as they will see through this tacky promotion.

Once again, look at the corporate giants—sale, sale, sale. Special offer after special offer. It always looks like they are coming up with a new promotion or idea.

If you don't currently have regular sales, perhaps you should start planning them. This week's special, this month's special etc. Like all promotions, there is no advantage to have ongoing sales if you don't tell your customers—so save some money for advertising.

A clever idea is to do a mail-out to your existing customers to let them know about the sale. Send them a card or a voucher of some sort that will enable them to come in before the general public to claim a discount.

94 The power of free samples

Always have free samples of your work or product on display. Think back to the last time you visited the local supermarket and someone pushed a plate of exotic sausages or cheese under your nose for a free trial. Or at the bottle shop for the Friday night free wine-tasting. Once again, if the large companies do this, you can be guaranteed that it works.

In America it is common to see people handing out samples of a new product like a chocolate bar or soap powder on Park Avenue in New York. To the manufacturers this is a cost-effective and high profile way to reach a lot of potential consumers within a certain area.

Of course, government regulations may stop you from doing this in some places, but try it inside your business. Do you remember going to the local butcher and receiving a few free sausages or perhaps half a kilogram of the latest stir-fry mix to take home and try? This type of marketing is very effective for a number of reasons:

- the customer receives something for free;
- the butcher has introduced a new range that the customer may not normally have tried but now they may include it in the weekly purchase; and
- the customer will come back to the butcher because they feel important and, to the butcher, they are.

I recently visited the local seafood shop to buy some prawns. When I walked in the door the very friendly man behind the counter put a big, juicy prawn on a napkin and handed it to me. The prawn was fantastic and of course I purchased a kilo. Everyone that walked into the shop was given a prawn in this manner and everyone that I saw purchased at least one kilogram of prawns.

I recently met a young man who had started up a courier business. He was charging the same price as the other couriers in town but on the tenth order he was giving away a bottle of champagne. This was a very clever idea. Generally secretaries book couriers; as prices are basically the same they can choose which company they use. Which company do you think they would use? Our company started using this courier straight away.

Remember the value of free samples. All businesses can supply some kind of free product or service as a sample. Use this as an introduction to a new client or as a way to keep your customers happy or as an incentive to purchase more.

95 Offer a second opinion for free

I recently came across an advertisement for a mechanical repair shop in the local newspaper. The advertisement had a big heading (which I love) that said, 'Are you sick of being ripped off by your mechanic?' This caught my eye and I read on to discover that this clever mechanic was offering a second opinion for free. If you had a quote from another mechanic you could take it to them and they would quote the job to make sure you weren't getting ripped off.

Imagine if the advertising mechanic's quote is cheaper than the one in your hand (which I am sure it always would be). Who is going to get the work? This is a great way to generate interest from customers in a very non-threatening way. The clever mechanic is inviting people to come to them to save money. I would get a second price on a big mechanical job—would you?

Just about any business that offers higher priced products or services can make this offer. Most consumers are aware that it pays to shop around. By putting the offer in black and white you are reminding the customer to shop around and hopefully your price will be better. Even if your price isn't better you get the customer into your business where hopefully they will be impressed enough to use your services anyway.

Another variation on this theme is that when a customer rings for a price it pays to always give them a good price but also to leave the inquiry open. Suggest that you may be able to do better if they want to buy it today or offer a discount if paying cash or perhaps if they intend to buy more than one item.

I always find it interesting when I ring a business for a price on something and they make no attempt to try and close the deal or to offer an enticement to encourage me to buy. A good way to help keep a person interested is to give them your name and invite them to talk to you personally if they require any further help. Perhaps your business can start offering free second opinions today.

96 What is 'value adding' and can you use it?

One of the buzz marketing terms of this decade is 'value adding'. What this means in simple terms is that rather than discounting your products to attract customers you value add the purchase by offering an extra service or product as part of the sale.

For example, imagine if you are a builder trying to sell houses in a new property development. You could offer a $10 000 discount on a house or land package or, alternatively, 'value add' the property by including a free pool.

Value adding has a number of advantages over discounting. First, it gives your business a point of differentiation over your competitors. If a price war erupts you can avoid it by value adding your products instead of joining the war.

What normally happens in price wars is that the company with the biggest cash reserves lasts the longest and everyone else goes broke. Price wars have no winners other than the consumers because businesses end up doing lots of work for no money. If you are not making money, why bother being in business?

The other advantage of value adding is that you can advertise the retail price of the add-on product, but in fact you would normally be paying wholesale. Using the builder example mentioned previously, a flat discount of $10 000 is exactly that—$10 000 in cold hard cash that you will no longer have. If you are offering a free pool to the value of $10 000, being a builder you would probably buy and install the pool for $7000. Hence you get the benefit of a $10 000 incentive that only costs $7000.

Another advantage of value adding is that it makes your customers feel they are getting something for free. They feel like winners. A happy customer will keep coming back.

There really are very few businesses that could not take advantage of value adding their products or services. Some examples include:

- accountant—free personal tax done with all business tax returns;
- restaurant—free dessert with any main course;
- mechanic—free wash and wax with any service;
- panel beater—free service with any body work;
- solicitor—free wills for all existing customers;
- hairdresser—free head and shoulder massage with every cut;
- builder—free garage with every house; and
- takeaway—free can of drink with every works burger.

More and more companies are value adding their products. A point to remember is that the value-added product or service needs to be attractive to the potential customer. If you are offering a really miserable value-added product, most people will stick with the other company offering the discount.

97 Using a 'gift with purchase' to sweeten the deal

I recently started buying computer supplies from a company by mail order. They constantly impress me not only with their excellent service but with the fact that they religiously pack a small box of chocolates with every order they send us.

This is a real treat. It is definitely out of the ordinary and I have to admit it is a very good marketing idea. For the sake of a few dollars, less if you buy in bulk, why not stand out from your competitors by offering a small gift when people make a purchase. Don't promote it—just do it and judge the response from your customers.

Once again, ask yourself how often you receive a gift in this manner. I would hazard a guess and say very rarely. If the choice is between you and the company up the road, a small box of chocolates could be all the difference.

Gifts can be anything that are either a treat or that have perceived value. I have made purchases from a few companies that always include a voucher for $10 with my order. This voucher entitles me to $10 off my next order. It is only a small saving but I use them because of the voucher— none of their competitors use the voucher system.

Increasing sales and keeping customers coming back are normally about the little things, not the big ones. If you are smart enough to have a company selling a product or service, the odds are reasonably good that you know what you are doing in your particular field. The important question to ask yourself is how do you rate in fields such as customer service and follow-up?

13 | Is your business promoted in as many places as possible?

This section details a few places to promote your business you may have overlooked. They are areas where we spend a lot of time and so do many other people. It also provides an outline on one of the oldest and most popular marketing tools—the magnet. As we come to the end of our 101 ways, we'll look at:

#98   An easy way for customers to keep your number handy

#99   The power of the local convenience store

#100   People read noticeboards in shopping centres

#101   Next time you visit the gym

98 An easy way for customers to keep your number handy

Fridge magnets are tried and tested as a great way for people to keep your telephone number handy. Most of the time the reason people don't bother using them is because they don't know who to ring to get them made up. Take a few minutes, pick up the Yellow Pages and get those fingers walking. There are hundreds of companies producing magnets in millions of varieties around the world and they are surprisingly inexpensive.

Try and come up with something a little bit unusual and eye-catching. Keep your company message simple—people understand how to order pizza, so if you run a pizza shop you only need to tell your customers the phone number, if you home deliver, and perhaps an address so they know that you are in their area. Make it colourful and it will attract attention.

Fridge magnets have thousands of applications and I would hazard a guess and say that there would be very few businesses that wouldn't be able to use this form of marketing. Who wouldn't want their company name under the nose of potential clients every day?

Our favourite florist has a fridge magnet they give out with every delivery. The local council made a fridge magnet with the customer service number printed on it. These were then delivered to every household in the area.

Another clever idea that I came across was four companies doing a joint cooperative marketing campaign by advertising on a fridge magnet about the size of a business card. All they had were their names and their telephone numbers but they had split the cost four ways. The companies involved included a Chinese restaurant, a real estate agent, a taxi company and an airline. All numbers that could be used reasonably regularly. Enough to warrant being put in a place of honour on the fridge.

99 The power of the local convenience store

Hundreds of people walk in and out of the corner store every day. They are people from all walks of life and maybe they are potential customers for your business. Why not ask the shop proprietor if you can leave your flyers or business cards somewhere in the shop? Or perhaps there is a noticeboard. If there isn't, maybe you could sponsor one.

Another idea is to have a regular competition that is run in conjunction with the local store. Periodically your business donates a prize and the competition is entered into by all customers visiting the store. This cooperative campaign means that your business gets the exposure and access to potential new customers and the store has happy customers. Perhaps a picture of the monthly winner is put up on the noticeboard.

While a promotion like this may seem small and insignificant, the biggest brand names in the world like Coca-Cola and Pepsi spend thousands of dollars on signage at these small stores simply because they know the benefits.

100 People read noticeboards in shopping centres

People read noticeboards in shopping centres. Put your company flyer or business card in the corner whenever you visit the local shopping centre. How much effort does this take?—about five minutes and a drawing pin. You may be surprised at the amount of business received from this simple promotion.

A friend of mine makes a comfortable living as a handyman. He markets his services by putting signs up on shopping centre noticeboards. He gets five to ten calls per week from each noticeboard and most turn into small jobs.

Handymen, gardeners, babysitters and cleaning businesses can virtually run their operations from noticeboards scattered throughout the region. If you keep a supply of business cards and flyers in your car you will never be caught out. It is also a good idea to keep a box of pins close by as these are normally in scarce supply on the actual noticeboards.

Quite often large shopping centres have shops vacant for a few months at a time. These shops are sometimes already leased but the tenant is not moving in immediately. This provides you with an opportunity to approach the centre and put up a permanent display promoting your business and the services you provide. Rent in this instance is normally minimal as it is often preferable to have a display of some sort rather than an empty shop.

Once again, this is a situation where it doesn't hurt to ask, but remember that if you are going to put a display into a shop or a shop window, make certain that it is high quality, professional and easy to understand. Make up a sign saying where your business is located and the hours that you operate and leave a supply of flyers or brochures for people to take.

If your business would conflict with other tenants in the centre, it is unlikely that you will be able to put a display in. Prepare a professional presentation folder with samples of your brochures and promotional material and be prepared to negotiate with the landlord.

I see this as a great opportunity for a group of small companies to promote themselves, such as a medical centre or a day care centre or a complete car care centre.

Friends of mine own a furniture manufacturing company. They approached a local shopping centre to put a display into a vacant shop at the front of the building. The lease was month-to-month and the rent was a flat 10 per cent of turnover of sales based out of the shop. My friends were considering renting a shop in a centre and committing to a lease. However, this gave them the opportunity to trial the idea at a minimal cost (the shop did not prove viable and they moved back to the factory showroom).

101 **Next time you visit the gym**

One idea I recently came across was at a local gym. This gym has over 1000 members. A number of businesses had sponsored a noticeboard where they made special offers to all of the gym members—all the members had to do was to show their membership card to claim the discount.

This struck me as a particularly clever way to target a good group of consumers. Most people that go to the gym would fall into a typical 18–35 year age bracket with a good disposable income (that can at least afford to pay membership and buy trendy clothes), making them a good target for a direct marketing campaign.

Being a member of a gym means that you would probably talk to other members as well, so news of a special deal or offer would travel quite quickly. The gym itself benefits from this promotion in that their customers receive a benefit for being a member of the gym. Once again, a situation that makes everyone a winner.

Another idea involved a company that paid for the membership cards to be produced and laminated. On the back of the card they had an advertisement. This was a sporting shop, which is obviously a good choice.

The same principle could apply to a fishing club, rifle club, gardening club or whatever. If your business is particularly complementary to a certain club, perhaps today is the day to pick up the phone and arrange a meeting.

Another 20 easy marketing ideas for your business

Just to prove that I practice what I preach, I have value added this book by including a bonus section containing twenty more marketing ideas. These are some of my favourites and they include straight marketing ideas as well as operational tips for increasing business.

#102   People expect and deserve fast service

#103   Make up a specific fax brochure

#104   Start your own club

#105   People do business with people they like

#106   Deal with customer complaints quickly and fairly

#107   Make your own company video

#108   Do a desktop publishing course

#109   Make an audio tape to promote your business

#110   Remember your customers' names

#111   Have a 'thank you' party for your customers

#112   Keep accurate customer records

#113   Most businesses don't follow up on sales leads

#114   Bribe your customers with food

#115   Write letters to the editor

#116   Arrange a business networking lunch

#117   Perseverance pays

102 **People expect and deserve fast service**

We are living in a world where everything is happening fast. Technology is moving at an incredible rate, scientific breakthroughs happen every day, fortunes are made and lost a hundred times per day. The current model is outdated the minute you leave the showroom.

What does this mean to the average person trying to sell products and services? It means a lot. Consumers' expectations have changed. Long delays in supplying goods or services are no longer acceptable. The old days of 'we will get it to you in a few weeks' are long gone. When we go through the drive-in at McDonald's we expect that burger to be in the car in a few seconds. If we are told that it is going to take more than a minute, we sit there impatiently, watching the clock, unhappy about the delay. How long would it take us to buy the ingredients for a burger, prepare and cook it? A lot longer than 60 seconds (especially if I am cooking it).

The same principle applies to your business. If you can't supply something quickly, whether it be a burger or a book, people will lose interest and go somewhere where they can get it—fast. Consumers want instant action.

Of course not all businesses can offer instant action. However, most businesses can improve the speed at which they operate. Some of the common faults that I see with businesses being slow are outlined below.

1. Slow telephone answering These businesses always take ten rings before they answer. Then the person who does answer is distracted because the phones are still ringing in the background so you don't get their full attention. These companies are obviously already very busy, but how much business are they losing because customers stop waiting for them to answer the phone?

2. Poor customer processing Some businesses just can't seem to get the hang of serving more than one customer at a time. I am amazed at how many large corporations don't seem to be able to do this either. If you always have a sea of people waiting at your counter, look at ways of speeding things up and making it more organised. Some banks offer a great service for business accounts where you put your deposit into an envelope and drop it into a special box. No waiting and no queuing. This saves our company a lot of time each week and, most importantly, we leave the bank saying what a great idea it is.

3. The 'we will have to order it in' business Some businesses never seem to have what you want in stock, but never fear, they can order it in and it will only take six weeks. Forget it—the sale is gone. Customers want it now. If you can't supply what they want they will go somewhere that can.

4. The 'I'll call you back' business These ones infuriate us all. The business that promises to call you when your order comes in or when it is repaired or to give you a quote and they never do.

From my experience, most of the above problems occur with companies that have grown rapidly. The business is having a hard time keeping up with the influx of new customers. Unfortunately, if they don't do something about their slow service, the number of new customers will slowly dwindle.

I am sure that your business would not fall down in all of the above, but maybe you could improve in a few areas. I recommend you conduct a 'speed audit' and see if there are ways you can provide a quicker service for your customers.

103   Make up a specific fax brochure

I often get faxes sent to my office that I can barely read. Someone has grabbed a copy of their company brochure and whizzed it through the fax machine in anticipation of me spending thousands of dollars with their company. I normally spend about five minutes trying to decipher a mass of text and pictures that mean absolutely nothing before the fax gets thrown into the recycled paper pile. As far as I am concerned it is a complete waste of time for me and the person who sent the fax and, in all honesty, I resent their business for blocking my fax machine and wasting my paper.

If you are serious about faxing people as a promotional tool, make up a specific flyer or letter that is designed to be faxed. To create a successful fax flyer, there are a few criteria you need to follow:

- Give it a big, catchy heading. Faxes are like any advertising—if you haven't got the reader's attention within a few seconds you are wasting your time.
- Don't try and fax pictures—they rarely come through clearly.
- Leave lots of white space in the fax.
- Make sure that type size is large enough to be read easily (I often get great faxes from companies but I can't read their contact numbers, so even if I wanted to buy their products, I couldn't).

The main point to this section is that if you are going to use the fax machine as a source of generating new business (which I highly recommend), take the time to design a flyer specifically for that purpose. Once you have made a 'fax brochure', send it to a few friends and get them to tell you if it works.

Another point worth mentioning are the companies that send you a fax with a dirty great line through the middle of it. This line, or lines, always obliterate an important message or a phone number. They take away from the overall quality of the fax. They are caused by bits of dirt on the scanning head of the facsimile sending the fax. All you need to do is wipe it off and the lines are gone. If you are not sure if your machine is making these lines, copy a piece of paper through the fax. If it comes out with a line through the middle then your fax is the culprit.

104 Start your own club

Why not start up your own club? Just about any business can do it, all you need is some time to devote to managing your club membership. The main benefit to your business of starting a club is that it keeps you in touch with your customers and it provides a way to encourage them to buy more products from you.

Clubs can take many shapes and forms. I have seen the local mechanic offering a club membership that entitles members to discounts on all mechanical work, a special waiting room for members only, which has special treats, and a monthly 'taking care of your car' newsletter that is used to sell new products. Membership is free and the incentives are great.

All of the major airlines offer clubs. These cost quite a bit of money to join but the privileges are good and the peace and quiet of an airline lounge far outweighs the noisy, crowded terminals.

I have a friend in a restaurant club where once a month all members are invited to the restaurant to try new meals before they go onto the menu. The members pay a reduced figure for the meal but they feel special because they are the first to try these new dishes. A wine company provides free samples for the night and everyone has a great time. The restaurant benefits from the word-of-mouth advertising as well as finding out if their proposed dishes are going to be popular before they put them on the menu.

Some department stores offer pre-sale shopping for club members. They send a letter to all of their club members explaining that they are having a sale starting on Saturday, but members can bring in the club card and they will receive their discounts three days before the sale. Hence club members are rewarded by having access to special items before everyone else.

To start a club you need to do a few simple things, including:

- decide on a name for the club;
- develop a regular newsletter;
- give people a reason to join (things like discounts, regular newsletters etc.);
- develop a membership card or some other form of identification; and
- decide whether membership is free or if there will be a yearly cost (I recommend that it should be free if you can afford it).

Forming a club may be a great way for you to create a loyal band of customers who will not only shop with you more regularly but will also tell their friends about this great club they are members of. Like all marketing ideas, your club will only work if you tell your customers about it. Make the information readily available and make joining simple. If the membership document is ten pages long, no one will join. All you really need are the customer's name, address, telephone number and email address.

I also find that it is important to reassure people that the information you collect will be kept confidential. Ironically, more people know more about what we do now than ever before.

If you have a website, try to encourage people to join the club via your site. This is a fairly simple procedure that any web designer could set up for you.

Managing your club membership details can become quite a job as numbers grow, so be prepared to set aside enough time to manage your database well.

105 **People do business with people they like**

This is another one of those basic human fundamentals. If given the choice between dealing with someone we like and dealing with someone we don't like, the choice is simple. The person we like wins hands down every time.

There is an old Chinese saying that states, 'A man without a smile should never open a shop'. I often come across people without smiles running businesses that rely on customers coming back time and time again. The problem is that the customers go in once, they leave depressed and they never come back again.

So how does this affect you? If you can't be happy and cheerful in your place of business, find someone who can be. We all have daily problems, whether it be a lack of money, a supplier who has let us down, a difficult customer or a fight with our spouse. The point is that you need to get over these problems and put yourself in the right frame of mind to create a warm and inviting place of business where people will want to shop.

I often recommend to clients that the best way for them to increase their business would be for them to stop serving at the counter. If they take my advice it normally works and they become happier. They don't have to deal with the public as much so when they do, they are generally more friendly and relaxed, resulting in a much better experience for all involved.

I know that many small businesses don't have the luxury of just running out and hiring extra staff because they feel tired and stressed out, but being irritable and grumpy behind the counter will cost you far more money in the long run. Working with the public is very demanding and we all need a break once in a while.

I often hear people saying things like, 'That's just the way I am' or 'I'm no good in the morning'. Whatever the reason for negativity, try to take positive steps to change it. Read some inspirational books (there are a number of titles suggested at the back of this book). Ask people who always appear friendly and chirpy how they do it. Look for ways to send out the right message and your business will benefit from it.

106 Deal with customer complaints quickly and fairly

At some stage in your business life you will have to deal with customer complaints. Very few businesses are good at handling complaints. The best outcome that can be achieved from a complaint is that the customer leaves on good terms and continues to use your business. The worst outcome is that the customer leaves the store vowing never to return, telling all of their friends how bad your business is. Obviously the first option is a lot better.

How many complaints are acceptable? Ideally, the obvious answer is none. In a perfect world we would all love to have no complaining customers. In reality this is unlikely to happen. It really is a numbers game where the more people you deal with the more likely you are to have the odd complaint.

There are a number of issues to address when it comes to dealing with complaints. First, what is a complaint? I believe they take various forms from the simple wrong item purchased to a faulty product or service to a broken promise or business arrangement. A complaint arises in any situation where the customers feel they have not got what they paid for and they voice their opinion by complaining to the business.

Prevention is better than a cure so try to make certain that your business is running smoothly to reduce the risk of customer complaints. Slow service is the thing I find the hardest to tolerate, especially in restaurants, bank queues or when waiting on the phone. If your business is getting complaints about one particular product or service, do yourself a favour and fix it up straight away.

The next step is to make up a customer complaints policy. This simply means that you will decide now how to deal with any complaints you receive. Your policy needs to be fair and reasonable and I suggest that, when it comes to a product a customer has purchased, you offer to exchange the product or refund the money without hesitation. Those businesses that refuse refunds are in some cases breaking the law, especially if the product is faulty. Design a complaints policy that is fair. If you are not sure how to approach this, talk to friends in business and ask them how they handle complaints. Once you have formulated a policy, make certain that your staff are aware of what it is.

Large department stores offer refunds immediately. Why? Because they know that the customer will keep shopping there because they have been fairly treated. Is it worth losing a regular, loyal customer over a few dollars?

If the complaint is more complicated, it is very important not to start arguing with the customer. If it starts turning ugly, no one wins and you may have to call in a mediator. From my experience I have found that the best way to handle a more complex complaint is to follow this procedure:

1. Keep calm and polite. Treat the complaint seriously.
2. Ask for all the details and write them down.
3. Ask the customer how they would like to see the problem resolved.
4. Tell the customer that you will look into their complaint and get back to them at a specific time.
5. Find out all the facts from your point of view.
6. Decide on a fair way to resolve the complaint.
7. Contact the customer at the exact time you said you would.
8. Advise them of all the facts from your point of view and what you are proposing to do to rectify the problem.
9. Ask the customer if they are happy with your suggestion for rectifying the problem. If they are not, negotiations will have to continue until an outcome is achieved.

10. Thank the customer for bringing the problem to your attention and ask them to contact you directly if they ever have a problem again.

Whenever you find yourself in the position of dealing with a customer complaint, always try to keep the desired end result in the back of your mind. You want the person making the complaint to continue being one of your customers so try to resolve the issue quickly, fairly and professionally. Don't tear yourself to pieces if you get the odd complaint. Keep an eye on your business to make certain that you are doing everything possible to keep complaints to a minimum.

107 **Make your own company video**

Once again, technological advances help out with this very visual marketing tool. A few years ago making a corporate video would cost a minimum of $10 000 for a ten- to fifteen-minute documentary featuring the services offered by your company. Today modern video equipment produces very high quality footage and can be purchased relatively inexpensively; it can even be hired for a small sum.

The advantage of making your own corporate video is that it enables you to really show a prospective customer what your business can offer them. As we all know, a picture tells a much better story than a hundred pages of writing.

When making your video you need to follow a few simple guidelines. First of all, plan exactly what you want to film. What message are you trying to give? Is the video a general one that shows all of the products and services you offer or is it more specific, featuring one particular aspect of your business?

Once this is decided you need to think about who will be in the video. There is nothing wrong with having your staff members featured and, in fact, I think it is good because it can show the human side to your company. You may want to set the video up in a nice room and have the staff members come in one by one to explain the role they play in the day-to-day running of the company.

Next you have to make sure that everything looks as clean and tidy as possible. Make sure that the factory is clean, the uniforms are ironed and the lawn cut. Little details can make all the difference when it comes to filming.

Lighting is also important. If you are filming outdoors try to do it early in the morning or late in the afternoon to get the best light. If you are filming indoors, try moving a few lights around to change the look of the room and to give the video a more professional feel.

Try to add a little humour. I know that I seem to keep harping on this point but we all appreciate a good laugh from time to time. If your video can bring a smile to someone's face, perhaps they will decide to buy some products from you.

Once you have filmed everything you will need to edit. This simply means cutting bits out and moving them around. You may want to do a voice-over or add commentary to a particular section. This can either be done by a friend who knows how to use their new computer or you may have to take it to a studio for editing. Places that can do this are found in the Yellow Pages under 'Video or television production' and most television stations also offer this service. It may cost a few hundred dollars but your video will look a lot more professional. The same places that edit the video can do reproductions for you so you order as many copies as you can afford at the time. You can also get loop tapes made that have the video repeated for up to four hours which makes it perfect for placing in a waiting room or shopfront.

You will also need to make a flyer to insert into the cover of the video. This can be done on any word processor. It may need to be trimmed to fit into the plastic cover. Try using a different colour paper for the insert. It will look better and add to the overall presentation of the video.

The next step is to hand them out to prospective customers. Ask them to spend a few minutes looking at the video to get a feel for the services your company offers. Try to keep it short—no more than 5 or 6 minutes at the most.

Another idea that I believe works well is to ask a few customers to give a brief testimonial on your video. Get them to tell people why they use your business. This can be very convincing and it adds an air of authenticity to your business.

Who knows, you may like filming so much that you close your business to pursue a new career in Hollywood. The worst that can happen is that you end up with a really good promotional tool that can be used in a variety of situations to spread the message about your business.

108 Do a desktop publishing course

Most small businesses have computers these days. In fact, it is hard to imagine any business getting by without one. With the computer revolution has come the software revolution. Programs are readily available that give anyone the resources to produce reasonably good flyers and promotional material. These programs are not necessarily expensive and they are getting easier to use. The problem is knowing what to do with them.

One of the best investments any small business operator can make is to sign up for a desktop publishing course. On these courses you will learn how to lay out a range of documents and promotional material that will really help you in marketing your business. These courses are offered all of the time in various institutes and private tuition is available in the classified section of most newspapers.

A desktop publishing course will not make you a graphic designer. These people are generally very skilled individuals who specialise in high quality artwork and promotional material. It will give you the ability to produce a range of flyers and simple brochures to promote your business. There are also excellent books available to teach you the basics of desktop design and layout.

I had never touched a computer until about seven years ago. Now all our promotional material is produced in-house. This not only saves money but it also gives us the freedom to design promotional items on the spur of the moment. With the advent of laptop computers you can make up a new brochure next time you visit the beach.

Desktop design is becoming an important skill for all small business operators. You can save a lot of money and improve your overall corporate image simply by learning a few basic skills.

109 **Make an audio tape to promote your business**

I see more and more companies doing this and I must admit that I like it. The only place I have spare time is in the car. Virtually every car has a cassette player so why not listen to a tape. I have started buying audio books so that on long trips I can 'read' a novel or a business book without the usual craziness of a busy office.

Why not make up a short tape outlining the services and products your business offers? Give it to a prospective client or customer and ask them to listen to it the next time they are in the car. You get most of their attention in a reasonably uninterrupted environment.

To make up a tape is not expensive. All you need is a tape recorder and a microphone. I suggest writing a bit of a script so that you present your story in a systematic manner. It is important that you let the information flow and try to avoid the monotone robotic voice. Be light and upbeat and try to add a little humour.

If you have the time, really personalise the message. Perhaps something like the following:

> Mr Jones, I would like to thank you for taking the time in your hectic schedule to listen to my proposal. I would really like your business and in the next few minutes I am going to tell you how our company can not only save you a lot of money but also provide you with a better end product . . .'

Another way to improve your chance of success is to make the package the tape is delivered in a little unusual. Perhaps with a bold message on the cover that the receiver couldn't miss.

I really do believe this is a great way to present your case to potential customers, particularly if they are difficult to get an appointment with. This saves you time and them time and hopefully you will put forward a compelling case to encourage them to give you the business.

110 **Remember your customers' names**

Every time I go into my local video shop I am cheerfully greeted by a number of people behind the counter who all know my name. I am not an outstanding customer who rents a thousand videos a week but I do go in there regularly. The staff at this video shop have made the effort to remember my name. When you spend a bit of time in the store you soon realise they have made the effort to learn the names of many of their customers.

I like it. Whenever I walk into this shop I always feel welcome and I appreciate the fact that I am no longer just another customer. I am someone important enough for the staff to make the effort to remember my name.

We all have customers we deal with a lot, sometimes on a daily basis, yet we don't make the effort to find out their name so that instead of a casual anonymous greeting we can actually say, 'Hi Bob'. If you have been dealing with each other for quite a while it may be embarrassing to ask their name (especially if they know yours), but forget pride, say you're sorry and ask for their name.

This familiarity can really change a relationship from simply business to a more personal interaction, which I believe ultimately increases business. Make it easy for people to know your name by making up name tags for you and your staff. If someone is making the effort to wear a name tag I always make the effort to use their name, once again making the interaction more personal. One of the greatest motivational speakers and writers of all time, Dale Carnegie, emphatically believed that the sweetest sound to any person was the sound of their own name.

Of course the hardest part of asking names is to remember which name goes with which face. A little trick I use when introduced to someone is to picture the face of a friend with the same name next to the face of the person I have just met. Whenever I see the 'new' person I get a quick picture of my old friend at the same time, thus allowing me to remember the correct name. It rarely fails and enables me to remember the names of a lot of people. You need to be disciplined and do this mental exercise straight away. Perhaps repeat it in your head a few times to make sure that it sticks.

Increase your business by taking the time to remember your customers' names.

111 Have a 'thank you' party for your customers

Throwing a party for your customers to say 'thanks for the business' is a fabulous way to create goodwill. It doesn't mean that you have to rent the penthouse at the Ritz and order cases of French champagne. It can be something as simple as drinks one afternoon after work.

The great thing about putting on a function like this is that it provides a stress-free way for you to mingle with your customers to personally thank them. It gives them the opportunity to see that you really do appreciate their business, emphasising the fact that, as customers, they are special.

I used to have a barbecue once a week in my dive shop. This was on Thursday nights and it was very informal, basically a sausage sizzle. Everyone who came could receive a free air fill and a meal with a few drinks. At its peak over 50 people would attend every week. That Thursday night became the week's highlight for many customers and the best part about it was that I sold more dive gear that night than at any other time during the week. People were relaxed and happy, they had got something for free and they were happy to buy my products.

If you host a thank you party for your customers you may be surprised at how much business you actually get on the night or the leads that will be generated for you to follow up in the following weeks.

When hosting a party like this try to keep the theme in line with your customers' likes and dislikes. A friend of mine owns a boatyard. If he hosted a party with light finger foods, champagne and classical music in the background he would probably have a limited turn up. Alternatively, another friend of mine owns an art gallery. If he put on a barbecue with beer and loud rock music playing, no one would attend his opening functions. So try to read your customers to make certain that you hit the mark right on.

As always, set your budget before the event to make certain you know how much it will cost you and make sure you can afford it. Then organise everything, send out the invitations (at least two weeks before) and go for it. Try to make a point of personally greeting everyone as they arrive.

112 **Keep accurate customer records**

One of my pet hates (yes, another one) is receiving a letter addressed to Mrs Andrew Gruffer. I throw these letters straight into the bin. If the person sending me this very important letter can't even get my name right then I don't want to do business with them.

The importance of keeping accurate customer records cannot be emphasised enough. Some companies seem to specialise in getting the details wrong. I get three letters every month from a company trying to sell me some financial services. Each letter is addressed to me in some way, but each one has my name spelt differently so the computer thinks it is three different people. This has been happening for years and I guarantee that I will never buy a thing from them because I know that to this company I am just a name on a list, not a potential valued customer.

Does your business keep good customer records? If it doesn't you should address the problem quickly. People are fairly understanding if you ring them to verify their details on your customer database as long as you tell them who you are and what you are doing.

If you run the type of business that regularly sends out information or newsletters to your customers, you will have a much greater response if you send it to the right person at the right address.

113 **Most businesses don't follow up on sales leads**

It is an unfortunate fact of life that most businesses don't follow up on leads. They may attend a trade show and have a thousand names to contact but they never do. I often find myself chasing companies that I am trying to buy things from. They make promises that they can never keep, they don't return phone calls, they don't send through quotes when they say they will, they don't provide the goods on time and so on.

From my experience, there are a lot of businesses like this. They spend a fortune on fitting out great shops and then spend another fortune on advertising, yet they are not organised enough to have a telephone enquiry followed up on or a possible lead generated.

I believe there are five main reasons for this. The first is that no one particular person is responsible for following up on leads. They often end up in a collective pool that floats from desk to desk until they are dropped into the bin. All leads should be given to an individual who should follow them through from start to finish.

The second reason is that businesses often don't have enough promotional material. A potential customer rings up and asks for information and prices about a product, but because typing up a letter and finding a brochure and mailing it all takes too long or the information is not available, it is forgotten.

In our business we keep a standard envelope pre-packed and ready for posting. It contains our company brochure, references from past clients, samples of work that we have done before and any information relevant to the customer's particular enquiry. Then all we have to do is to attach a brief cover letter and pop it in the mail. This makes an enquiry a two-minute job rather than an hour-long process.

The third reason is that businesses often don't know what to do with a lead when they get it. Should they ring the person or should they send them a letter or should they send them a fax? It really does depend on the individual situation. If you are not comfortable with talking to someone on the phone, drop them a line but make sure you include some promotional material about your company.

Keep it simple and make it relevant. If the lead was generated at a trade show mention this fact. Use some of the tips mentioned in this book to make contact with these potential customers. Another point to remember here is that it will often take more than one letter to get a results, so be prepared to have a series of follow-up letters ready, encouraging the potential customer to buy from you.

The fourth reason for people not following up on leads is simply that they are too busy. If this is the case in your business you may be losing a lot of money. Perhaps it is worth employing that extra person on a casual basis simply to process sales leads. This will free up your time and take some of the pressure off you.

I recently employed a very talented lady to spend one day per week generating new business. Linda has a good sales background and as a new mother she is quite content to only work a day or two every week. Her only job is to look for business opportunities and new clients that would suit our business. This is a great relief to me because I can spend more time processing the work I have to do and less time looking for new business.

The final reason for businesses not following up on leads is simply that people are not organised. They lose bits of paper with important messages, they forget things they have to do, they can never find the information required and they are in a constant state of 'getting back to you'. The only way to fix this problem is to get organised.

So the point to this section is to determine if leads are being followed up in your business and if they are not, identify why not and then do something about it.

114 Bribe your customers with food

One of the best ways I have found to be remembered and to generate business is to deliver food. I used to have a job that required me to call on travel agents in large cities around the world. I would always take some chocolates or buy some cakes or biscuits before arriving. I have yet to meet a business that turns you away when you come bearing mouth-watering treats.

I would really go out of my way to buy fantastic food that my customers would be very impressed with. Most sales representatives make the mistake of buying cakes around the corner from the business they are visiting. The problem with this is that every other sales representative buys their cakes from the same shop so the people receiving the cakes eventually get sick of them. I used to purchase my cakes from one bakery in each city. I would pre-order the day ahead and get them to deliver the cakes packed as requested to my hotel. Then I would load up the car and go for it. This ensured that wherever I went the cakes were different to the ones they normally received and they noticed this small point.

If cakes were too hard I would take boxes of chocolates or party packs of lollies. In summer I would buy a tub of ice-cream and some fruit to make up banana splits. For one presentation I took in a blender with tropical fruit and cocktail glasses. I made everyone a tropical cocktail. All of these ideas worked well and the more I got to know the individual customers the more radical my idea could become. I had a lot of fun and whenever I rang up to say I was coming to town I was welcomed with open arms and every one of my customers said that they loved it when I visited. As a pleasant side effect, the business our company received from each of the travel agents I visited steadily grew.

Another idea I implemented was to send our major clients a box of mangoes for Christmas. The area where I live is well known for producing the best mangoes in the world. They are at their best at Christmas time so it seemed logical to send a case as gifts to important customers. A box of mangoes costs about $10 and the airfreight to send them nationally is about $20. So for about $30 you have the perfect corporate gift that is opened in the office and everyone can enjoy it. Plus it shows that you have put some thought into your gift, not just made the standard purchase of a hamper or a bottle of cheap wine.

A friend of mine used to own a small dive boat. Most of the business he received was from tour booking desks and hotel concierges. Every Christmas his wife would bake about 50 fabulous Christmas cakes and they would spend a few days delivering them to the booking agents as a way to say thanks for their support during the year.

I believe this is a very important point. It is better to do something special, such as make your own cakes or go out of your way to buy special pastries and cakes, rather than go the cheap and nasty way. Every Christmas we are given bottles of wine and spirits from media representatives and printers that our business deals with. Of the fifteen bottles received last year thirteen were the cheapest wine you could buy. This has a negative effect and I believe these companies would have been better off not bothering with such tacky gifts.

One company gave us a cheap bottle of wine but they made it a great gift by relabelling it. They had taken a photo of all the staff at their recent Christmas party, which happened to be fancy dress, and had it made into labels. They renamed the bottle as 'Rot Gut' and put a very humorous 'how to use' instruction list on the back. They had turned a cheap, tacky bottle of wine into a great gift. The other bottles we were given ended up being thrown away (only one bottle was well worth drinking).

Why not pop in with morning tea for a prospective client? Put your letter or promotional material in with your treats to make sure you get acknowledged for what you have done. I have heard of people sending pizzas to prospective clients with their promotional material attached.

As a lover of fine foods this marketing idea has worked very well for me. Perhaps you can incorporate it into your marketing strategy. Target one business every week with a special treat of some sort. You might just be surprised at how much business you can generate with a few doughnuts.

115 **Write letters to the editor**

I always scan through the 'letters to the editor' section in the newspaper and I often notice the same people write in time and time again. One day it dawned on me that these people are getting great exposure for absolutely no cost at all. By taking the time to write a letter on their company letterhead they have voiced their opinion in a very public place. It can show that they are an authority in a particular field and that they care enough to take the time to voice their opinions.

There are a few simple steps to take that will increase your chances of having the letter published. There are also a few guidelines to follow to ensure that you don't write the wrong thing, resulting in bad publicity for your business.

- Keep you letter brief and to the point.
- If you quote facts and figures say where this information comes from.
- Don't be emotive. Write in a simple, clear manner that shows you know what you are talking about.
- Remember that your letter may be edited so write it in a way that will make it hard for sentences to be cut, resulting in a change to the meaning of what you are trying to say.
- Be topical. If you are writing in response to an article that was published in the paper, do it quickly. It loses all relevance if you send a letter in three months after the event.
- Always make sure you include your company name at the end of the letter.

This is one of those ideas that doesn't cost any money but can produce results. You don't have to stop at newspapers. Most magazines welcome letters from readers as do many websites. There has never been a better time to lock yourself in the office and start hammering the word processor keys.

You don't need to be a fabulous writer to send a letter to a newspaper or magazine so don't worry about that side of things. Just write the best letter you can and send it in promptly.

116 Arrange a business networking lunch

Business networking lunches are not a new idea; however, they can be a very good way to meet people and to make contacts that can provide your business with a boost. We all have a few friends in business who in turn have a few friends who can be invited. Perhaps arrange a guest speaker paid for by a small contribution from everyone attending.

The most important point to remember when attending networking functions is to do just that—network. Make sure you have a pocket full of business cards and a pen (good for jotting down notes on the back of cards after people have given them to you).

If you arranged the lunch, try to give it a theme and encourage people to communicate and mingle. If you are simply going to the lunch to drink too much and have the afternoon off then you can expect zero business. If you are going there hungry for business, so to speak, work the room. Be polite and friendly and talk to as many people as possible. If you are shy try to find someone who isn't and stick with them. Work together to cover the room. If you meet someone who has absolutely no possibility of providing you with business, don't walk away mid-sentence. Be polite, pick your time and use the excuse of having to go and generate some business to break away and move onto a person with more potential.

I know this may seem like a very mechanical situation, but the reality is that networking functions are places to source business. Networking is a term that has become a buzz word in the past ten years, to the point where we may cringe whenever we are invited to a business networking function. Regardless of that, it is without doubt one of the best ways to source new business and establish stronger ties with existing customers.

117 **Perseverance pays**

My 13-year-old nephew recently came to stay for a short holiday and one of the activities that I was roped into was ten pin bowling. The last time I visited the local ten pin bowling alley it was a graveyard. The person behind the counter was completely disinterested, the actual building was a mess and the few people that were there looked like the walking dead. This was about two years ago.

When I visited the same bowling alley this time the transformation was simply amazing. First of all, we didn't bother to make a booking because I thought no one would be there, especially on a Monday morning. Was I wrong. The place was jam-packed. As soon as we walked in the door someone came up to us and welcomed us to their bowling alley. We were then taken to the counter where a friendly and highly efficient lady told us all of the specials they had on offer at the moment. Within a few minutes we were bowling like troopers with free ice-creams, drinks, a voucher for a free lesson at any time we wanted as well as a discount voucher for the next time we played.

They got us to enter a competition to win a television and video and as a result they collected our names and addresses so they could contact us at a later date. Very clever.

I was somewhat shell-shocked but it just kept getting better. After a few gutter balls (by me, not by my nephew), a friendly gentleman appeared and whispered a few hints into my ear. It didn't help my score but that was my lack of skill, not his advice. I continually looked around this business and all I could see were smiling faces and happy people. By the way, they had also put in a child-care facility to encourage parents with small children to bowl.

This was now a booming business. What changed? The answer is simple. The people running this business obviously made a firm decision to turn this business around by trying as many things as they possibly could to make it easy for people to bowl, to make it fun and to give people a reason to come back. From a marketing point of view they were doing everything right.

The moral to this story is that you have to try to do lots of things to make your business work. If they all work you will end up with a thriving business. It probably won't happen overnight but it will happen. If you know of a business that seems to be booming, pay them a visit. Stop and have a good look around and see if they are doing all of the right things.

118 Send money to get attention

It is always hard to get someone's attention with a letter, especially if you are trying to sell them something. I have seen (and discussed earlier) a number of cute ideas, such as attaching a tea bag and starting the letter with 'Enjoy a cup of tea while you read this letter'. The problem can be that it is done to death. In the space of one week I received about ten letters with tea bags attached. While I think it is a great idea (and my shopping bill was cut down dramatically that week), why not try to be a little more creative?

A clever idea I discovered recently was based on attaching a coin to a letter. Stick it right slap bang in the middle of the page. A gold coin looks great but a silver one will do. You start your letter off with a big bold heading like:

Do you earn the equivalent of $249 600 per year?
Because that is what I would like to pay you to read this letter. It will take about 30 seconds for you to read the attached letter. I would like to pay you $1 for your 30 seconds. That is the equivalent of $2 per minute or $120 per hour or $4800 per week or $249 600 per year. It really is 30 seconds well spent.

Now that you are on the payroll, here is what I would like to tell you about . . .

Now this idea works for two reasons. The first is that it will definitely stand out from every other piece of junk mail that we receive on a daily basis and second, who could resist reading the attached letter after an introduction like that? I am sure the odd cynic would put their hand up but, believe me, the vast majority of people couldn't help but read a letter as unusual as this.

Of course you could face the problem that after a while everyone will be doing it but the best way to avoid that particular problem is to be the first. If you want to do a small, focused direct mail campaign to a few prospective clients, this is one way that will surely get their attention.

119 **Advertising in magazines**

Most magazines are published to cater for specific people with specific interests. This means that you can target the audience you are trying to reach. For example, if you own a SCUBA diving shop that sells diving equipment, it makes sense to advertise in a SCUBA diving magazine. This may seem obvious but it is a point that is often overlooked.

Another prime example of this is the adventure tour companies and environmental lodges that advertise in outdoor and nature-based magazines. The type of person who reads these magazines is probably very likely to enjoy outdoor activities and nature-based holidays, otherwise why buy the magazine?

Most magazines have small classified sections in the back exclusively for the smaller advertisers. Quite often you can place an advertisement for only a few hundred dollars. All you need to do is ring the publication (the details are always listed at the front of the magazine) and ask for details on advertising. The company will send you information called demographics, which outline the type of people that read this particular publication, where it sells the best, circulation numbers and advertising rates.

From here on it is up to you to decide how much you can afford and what service or product you want to promote in the advertisement. As with any printed media, remember that success is found in a clear, hard-hitting title. The magazine will help run through the requirements for your advertisement.

An observation I have made is that you normally see the same advertisements time and time again in specialist publications. This must lead to the assumption that they work.

If you want to monitor the success of the advertisement, either check with each and every customer to find out how they heard about your business or, alternatively, make up an offer that is exclusive to readers of that particular magazine, which involves either a cut-out coupon or special price that they quote.

120 **Can you generate more income with only a little extra effort?**

My accountant recently introduced me to an idea that I believe has merit for many other types of businesses. He explained that, due to a general tightening up by the taxation department, a proportion of his clients were audited every year. It wasn't anything out of the ordinary, it was just the way things were going. It was fair to assume that if you were in business you would be audited at some time in the future.

When a client is audited there are lots of expenses, especially the bill from their accountant who has to spend a lot of time sorting out records and answering the questions raised by the taxation department. So on top of the fine they may receive, the client also receives a bill for several thousand dollars from their accountant. All in all it is a very unpleasant experience for all involved.

My accountant introduced 'audit insurance'. What this basically means is that as a client you can pay a couple of hundred dollars per year and if you are audited all of your accounting bills will be covered by this insurance. Due to the increased possibility of being audited, this appears to me to be excellent value.

My accountant funds this insurance himself. All of the money raised from the policies goes into a pool. If he has a lot of clients audited he may lose out, but if he only has a few he tends to make a few dollars. In reality everyone wins. As a client, I have the peace of mind of knowing that when I am audited I don't have to worry about being hit with a large accounting bill at the end of the process. I also believe that this is a great service being offered and if my accountant makes a few dollars, well, good on him for having the initiative to put the plan in place.

Perhaps there are ideas like this that your business could put into place that could not only generate extra income for your business but also offer a degree of peace of mind for your customers. I have had friends in the car hire industry who say that often they make more money out of the insurance than they do out of hiring the car.

The key here is that you are taking some of the risk away from your customers and taking that responsibility on yourself—for a fee.

I went on a whale watching trip out of Boston in the USA several years ago. The company made a bold statement. If you don't see any whales they will refund half of your money. This seemed like a fair deal and as none of their competitors made the same offer I went with them and we saw about thirty whales. I was told they see whales every trip without fail, making this a fairly safe offer on their behalf.

I saw a similar insurance idea in Borneo where you could go on a fishing trip for about $100. You could then pay an extra $10 and if you didn't catch any fish you got all of your money back. They had self-insured themselves. I got to know the owner during the day and I asked him how many people had claimed the insurance. He said five people in ten years had claimed the refund ('they couldn't catch fish in a barrel with a bazooka'), yet almost 90 per cent of all his passengers paid the extra $10 for the insurance. This smart entrepreneur had increased his revenue by 10 per cent for a very minimal outlay. This doesn't take into consideration those people that went fishing on his point simply because he offered the novel insurance.

On another nautical theme, I remember going diving in Vanuatu once where you could take out clear water cover. If the water visibility dropped below 20 metres you dived for free. This premium cost about $20 per day, but as a mad keen diver how could I refuse this offer? Once again the owner said that occasionally bad weather made them give away some free dives, but overall they won out hands down as the visibility was normally well in excess of

50 metres. They had increased their revenue by almost 25 per cent simply by introducing this insurance policy.

The only real danger in this area is making certain that you are very, very clear about what the insurance covers and how you will measure it. As my accountant said, if I came to him smoking Cuban cigars and carrying suitcases full of small unmarked bills, he would probably be asking for trouble. Make your offer clear. Remember that if you are taking money from people they will be expecting something in return. Be certain to give it to them.

On the bright side, perhaps you could increase your business considerably simply by offering a new service or a type of insurance that really wouldn't cost you a lot in time or money.

121 Specialise

Another common mistake with many small businesses is that they try too hard to offer too many services and products. Over the years they end up doing so many different things that they get confused and they lose focus. I hate to think how their customers must feel.

I spend a lot of time trying to get our clients to simplify their businesses to make them easier to market. Put less information in your advertisements, simplify your promotional material, unclutter the shop and constantly look at your business through the eyes of a customer.

Whenever our company takes on a new client we have a brief meeting to get to know each other. The first question asked is, 'What does your business do—exactly?' After half an hour we have a list of all of the services and products available. At first the list is impressive but how do you tell people about it in a simple way?

One of our most complicated customers is a telecommunications firm that sells phone cards, cheap long distance calls, Internet access and so on. I often laugh with the owner because his business changes ten times every day. The telecommunications industry is so volatile that prices are never the same two days in a row and new products flood the market daily.

All we can do is pick one aspect of the business and develop a marketing plan for that product or service. Over the next few years we will have them all addressed but it is a long slow haul that is incredibly frustrating to all involved. Even the staff are not aware of all the products the company offers so, once again, what chance do their customers have?

I have made the same mistake in my business where I have tried to do too many things, to offer too many services and I rarely made money. As soon as I focused and began to specialise, my business became profitable.

Appendix:
Blank forms that may
come in handy

The following forms have been designed to illustrate a number of ideas raised in this book. Feel free to adapt them for use in your business.

Targets and Goals

How much business do we need every day?

....

....

....

....

....

....

How much business do we want every day?

....

....

....

....

....

....

How much business can we process every day?

....

....

....

....

....

....

....

Be Unique

Why should someone buy something from your business?

Take a few minutes to answer the above question and to identify what makes your business unique. Once you have done this, circulate the answer to your staff and your customers. This provides a clear reason for people to buy your products and services.

....

....

....

....

....

....

....

....

....

....

....

....

....

....

....

....

....

....

....

....

....

Big Titles

always get the customer's attention

Big titles always grab people's attention. Try to ensure that whenever you produce a flyer or an advertisement, you spend 90 per cent of your time working on the title and the rest of your time on the rest of the flyer.

Try to leave as much white space as you can in the document as well. Make your text neat and symmetrical. Try to limit the amount of information you are including in your promotional material.

Big titles always grab people's attention. Try to ensure that whenever you produce a flyer or an advertisement, you spend 90 per cent of your time working on the title and the rest of your time on the rest of the flyer.

Try to leave as much white space as you can in the document as well. Make your text neat and symmetrical. Try to limit the amount of information you are including in your promotional material.

Try to leave time working on the title and the rest of your time on the rest of the flyer.

Try to leave as much white space as you can in the document as well. Make your text neat and symmetrical. Try to limit the amount of information you are including in your promotional material.

Big titles always grab people's attention. Try to ensure that whenever you produce a flyer or an advertisement, you spend 90 per cent of your time working on the title and the rest of your time on the rest of the flyer.

Try to leave as much white space as you can in the document as well. Make your text neat and symmetrical. Try to limit the amount of information you are including in your promotional material.

Big titles always grab people's attention. Try to ensure that whenever you produce a flyer or an advertisement, you spend 90 per cent

COMPANY LOGO

INVOICE

Use your invoice to sell your business

Invoice Details	Amount
COMPANY LOGO	

NEWS FLASH—SAVE PLENTY

Use this space to promote your business and tell your customers about new products, special offers and general information about your business. Invoices are often passed through many hands and ultimately can be read by the person signing the cheques.

Sample customer survey for restaurants

Conducted by: .... Date: ....

1. **Do you live** ☐ Locally ☐ Within 50 kms ☐ Within 100 kms

2. **How did you get to our restaurant?** ☐ Bus ☐ Taxi ☐ Drove ☐ Walked

3. **Is this your first visit to our restaurant?** ☐ Yes ☐ No

4. **How did you hear about our restaurant?** ....

   ....

5. **Please rate the following:**

   A. Our telephone service ☐ Very good ☐ Good ☐ Average ☐ Poor

   Comments ....

   B. Quality of our products ☐ Very good ☐ Good ☐ Average ☐ Poor

   Comments ....

   C. Our prices ☐ Very good ☐ Good ☐ Average ☐ Poor

   Comments ....

   D. Our facilities ☐ Very good ☐ Good ☐ Average ☐ Poor

   Comments ....

6. **Would you eat at our restaurant again?** ☐ Yes ☐ No ☐ Maybe

   Comments ....

7. **Do you have any suggestions for improving our restaurant?**

   Comments ....

   Age: ☐ Under 18 ☐ 18–25 ☐ 26–35 ☐ 36–50 ☐ 50+

   Gender: ☐ Male ☐ Female (this section is optional)

PRESS RELEASE

27 July 2001

Local company knocks out competition

A local demolition company has knocked out all competitors by winning a national award for excellence. 'Designer Demolitions' have been operating for over 10 years, working on projects ranging from removing derelict houses to demolishing old highrise complexes. The award is based on an industry-wide survey that assesses all companies on their level of service, safety records, pricing, advertising and marketing and overall quality control.

Designer Demolitions owner and manager, Mr John Doe, stated '. . . this award recognises the hard work and effort put in by every single person working in this company. We take our demolishing seriously and I feel that we have received recognition for being the best in a tough and competitive industry.'

The award for Demolisher of the Year will be awarded to Mr Doe at a function later in the year. Mr Doe stated that '. . . all of the management and staff will celebrate winning this award at a party being held at head office in two weeks. Believe me, this party will have a few surprises.'

For more details please contact Carolyne Smith, the Director of Marketing for Designer Demolitions on telephone 343 4434 or facsimile 343 4343. After hours please call mobile 0454 344 434.

Corporate Image

Having a strong corporate image is very important. Make sure that you are giving your customers the right message. When planning your corporate image remember the following:

- Choose a colour or colours and use them consistently
- Use a specific typeface in all material
- Strong headings on all brochures and flyers
- Tell people why your business is different
- Be proud, fly your own flag
- Use pictures of people
- Keep it simple and uncomplicated
- Don't try and be too clever
- Make it easy for customers to contact you
- Use testimonials from satisfied customers
- Use quality paper—for a few cents more it makes all the difference
- Attention to detail—never rush production of promotional material

Your corporate image should flow through the following areas:

- Company brochures
- Outdoor signage
- Staff uniforms
- Company vehicles
- Websites
- All advertising
- Business cards

Marketing Activity

Date: ....

Marketing idea: ....
....
....

Budget: ....
....
....

Time frame to action: ....
....
....

Staff notified: ....
....
....

Results: ....
....
....
....

Comments: ....
....
....

Recommended reading

Bruber ME, 1995 *The E Myth Revisited*, HarperCollins, New York

Caples J, 1997 *Tested Advertising Methods*, Prentice Hall Business Classics, New Jersey

Carnegie D, 1981 *How to Win Friends and Influence People*, HarperCollins, New York

Covey S, 1990 *The 7 Habits of Highly Effective People*, Simon & Schuster, New York

Kehoe J, 1991 *Money, Success and You*, Zoetic Inc., West Vancouver

Levinson J & Godin S, 1994 *The Guerrilla Marketing Handbook*, Houghton Mifflin Company, New York

Matthews A, 1997 *Follow Your Heart*, Seashell Publishers, Cairns

Pritchard B, 1997 *Marketing Success Stories*, Milner Books, Burra Creek, Australia

White S, 1997 *The Complete Idiot's Guide to Marketing Basics*, Alpha Books, New York

About the author

Andrew Griffiths is an entrepreneur with a passion for small business. From humble beginnings as an orphan growing up in Western Australia, Andrew has owned and operated a number of successful small businesses, starting with his first enterprise—a newspaper round—at age seven. Since then Andrew has sold encyclopaedias door-to-door, travelled the world as an international sales manager, worked in the Great Sandy Desert for a gold exploration company and been a commercial diver. Clearly this unusual menagerie of experiences have made him the remarkable man he is.

Inspired by his desire to see others reach their goals, Andrew has written five hugely successful books with many more on the way. His 101 series offers small business owners practical and achievable advice. The series is sold in over forty countries worldwide.

Andrew is the founding director of The Marketing Professionals, one of Australia's best and most respected marketing and business development firms. Producing innovative solutions to common business issues, The Marketing Professionals advise both large and small business alike.

Known for his ability to entertain, inspire and deliver key messages, Andrew is also a powerful motivational speaker who brings flamboyancy and verve to the corporate keynote-speaking circuit.

All of this occurs from his chosen home of Cairns, North Queensland, the Great Barrier Reef, Australia.

To read more about Andrew Griffiths visit:
www.andrewgriffiths.com.au
www.themarketingprofessionals.com.au
www.enhanceplus.com.au